ARCHITECTURE ASIA

T0277793

Journal of the Architects Regional Council Asia (ARCASIA)

Editorial Team

WU Jiang
Editor in Chief

LI Xiangning
Vice Editor in Chief

ZHOU Minghao
Managing Editor

WANG Ying
Executive Editor

WANG Yanze
Executive Editor

WEN Huajing
Assistant Editor

ZHENG Xin
Assistant Editor

Contact
archasia@foxmail.com

Co-Publishers

The Architectural Society of China (ASC)
9 Sanlihe Road, Beijing, China, 100835

Tongji University
1239 Siping Road, Shanghai, China, 200092

Sponsor

Tongji Architectural Design (Group) Co., Ltd.
1230 Siping Road, Shanghai, China, 200092

Editorial Board

Abu Sayeed M. Ahmed
University of Asia Pacific, Bangladesh
President of ARCASIA

Russell Dandeniya
RDC Architects, Sri Lanka
Vice President of Zone A, ARCASIA

Ana S. Mangalino-Ling
JSLA Architects, Philippines
Vice President of Zone B, ARCASIA

Chun Gyu Shin
CGS Architects and Associates, South Korea
Vice President of Zone C, ARCASIA

KONG Yuhang
Tianjin University, China
Appointee from publisher

CAO Jiaming
The Architectural Society of Shanghai, China
Appointee from publisher

WU Jiang
Tongji University, China
Editor in Chief

LI Xiangning
Tongji University, China
Vice Editor in Chief

Stefano BOERI
Politeconico in Milan, Italy
External advisor proposed by publisher, approved by ARCASIA

Advisory Board Members

Ashutosh Kr AGARWAL
Ashutosh Kr Agarwal Architects, India

BOON Che Wee
GRA Architects Sdn Bhd, Malaysia

CHANG Ping Hung
Hong Kong University, Hong Kong, China

Calvin CHUA
Spatial Anatomy, Singapore

Apurva Bose DUTTA
Independent writer, architecture journalist, editor, India

Kenneth FRAMPTON
Columbia University, USA

HENG Chye Kiang
National University of Singapore, Singapore

Hilde HEYNEN
University of Leuven, Belgium

Kazuo IWAMURA
Tokyo City University, Japan

Juwon KIM
Hongik School of Architecture, South Korea

Min Seok KIM
Notion Architecture, South Korea

George KUNIHIRO
Kokushikan University, Japan

LEE Chor Wah
Former editor in chief of *Architecture Asia* and *Architecture Malaysia*, Malaysia

Shiqiao LI
University of Virginia, USA

Peter ROWE
Harvard University, USA

Nabah Ali SAAD
Lahore Campus, Pakistan

Khadija Jamal SHABAN
Smart Project Development, Pakistan

Nuno SOARES
Urban Practice Ltd., Macau, China

TAN Beng Kiang
National University of Singapore, Singapore

WANG Jianguo
Southeast University, Academician of Chinese Academy of Engineering, China

Johannes WIDODO
National University of Singapore, Singapore

WONG Ying Fai
The Hong Kong Institute of Architects, Hong Kong, China

Charlie Qiuli XUE
City University of Hong Kong, Hong Kong, China

Jianfei ZHU
Newcastle University, UK

ZHUANG Weimin
Tsinghua University, Academician of Chinese Academy of Engineering, China

Contents

Editorial

Lately, there has been a considerable exchange of ideas, cultures, and architectural designs among Asian countries touched by globalization; in fact, some of these exchanges actually go way back to an earlier time. However, despite the many alterations brought on by globalization, the different geographical and cultural backgrounds of some Asian countries and regions have allowed them to retain their native uniqueness to form a unique regional identity.

Against this backdrop, this issue points out some notes of interest.

1) The exchange and spread of Japanese architectural culture in China:
Zhu Xiaoming and Tian Guohua's article highlights how the badminton gymnasium designed by renowned Japanese modernist architect Kikuji Ishimoto in 1942, which forms part of a former Japanese school on Tongji University's Siping Road campus in Shanghai, crosses cultural and temporal boundaries and provides substantial evidence on the practice of early Japanese modernist architects in China.

2) Some of the common problems faced by Asian cities, such as congestion, poor environmental conditions, shortage of green areas, and poor use of public spaces are given local solutions:
Souporni Paul and Suchandra Bardhan's research investigates the spatial distribution of urban greening strategies and also discusses specific greening strategies in the Indian city of Kolkata at its smallest administrative unit, providing a local sample for this common issue.
Focused on matters on Shanghai, China's home front, the article by Gu Zhuoxing and team elaborates how a multi-agent behavioral simulation method was utilized to measure the use of public space in the North Bund waterfront to reveal that the public space in the North Bund has an uneven distribution of activities, activity time, and space utilization, and thereby suggests improvements in the overall space utilization.

3) Investigation and respect for locality:
Li Minqian and Li Xiaofeng's research focusing on traditional Yi settlements in Yunnan, China, proposes specific construction strategies for the revitalization of villages by activating shared space, including spatial scene design strategies at the village, group, and household levels, as well as the "mother tongue construction" strategy.

The project section in this issue provides varied alternative responses to address the topic of maintaining locality amid globalization. Asian architects interpret locality from various perspectives, not only regionally, but also universally. MoMA, Lushan Times, and Suzhou Urban Planning Exhibition Hall each reply to their complex urban surroundings with an outstanding and independent outlook. Office Complex for Gopal Printpack Solutions, Maly Koncert, and Zhongguancun Digital Economy Innovation Industry Base present investigations into ontological design from the perspective of internality. Wanping Theater, Rane Vidyalaya, and Athenia High School explicate innovative materials from indigenous culture. This issue highlights both the significance of Asian discourse in globalization, as well as its inherent responsibility for locality.

A Timber Gymnasium: Renowned Modernist Architect Kikuji Ishimoto's Early Works in 1940s Shanghai

ZHU Xiaoming, Tongji University, China
TIAN Guohua, Shanxi University, China

Abstract

The historic building cluster located at Tongji University's Siping Road Campus of Tongji University, which makes up a former Japanese school, was bestowed the Shanghai Outstanding Modern Architecture accolade by the Shanghai municipal government in 2005. The badminton gymnasium of this school was designed by renowned Japanese modernist architect Kikuji Ishimoto in 1942. He was a leading member of the Secessionist Architects Organization and studied at Bauhaus-Universitat Weimar with Master Gropius. Against the backdrop of World War II, he executed the concept of the gymnasium by carrying the potential of the wood structure into modernism.

This paper attempts to interpret the impact on architecture that the history of the campus has had, and with due diligence, also points out that in the 1990s, Japanese schools were demolished in large numbers in Shanghai due to rapid urban development, so only a few are still completely preserved. The badminton gymnasium is one such that falls within this narrow category of salvage, but has, unfortunately, long lacked attention. It is a large-span timber building which crosses cultural and temporal boundaries, providing further evidence on the practice of early Japanese modernist architects in China. Adding to that, it must also be noted that the badminton gymnasium is not an isolated structure, but part of the former Japanese secondary school. Its site has an important symbolic position that has been, regrettably, neglected in the evolution of urban space in Shanghai.

Author Information
ZHU Xiaoming: miaoxueyang@126.com
TIAN Guohua: tianguohuasxty@163.com

Keywords

Tongji University badminton gymnasium, Shanghai former Japanese secondary school, Kikuji Ishimoto, portal frame.

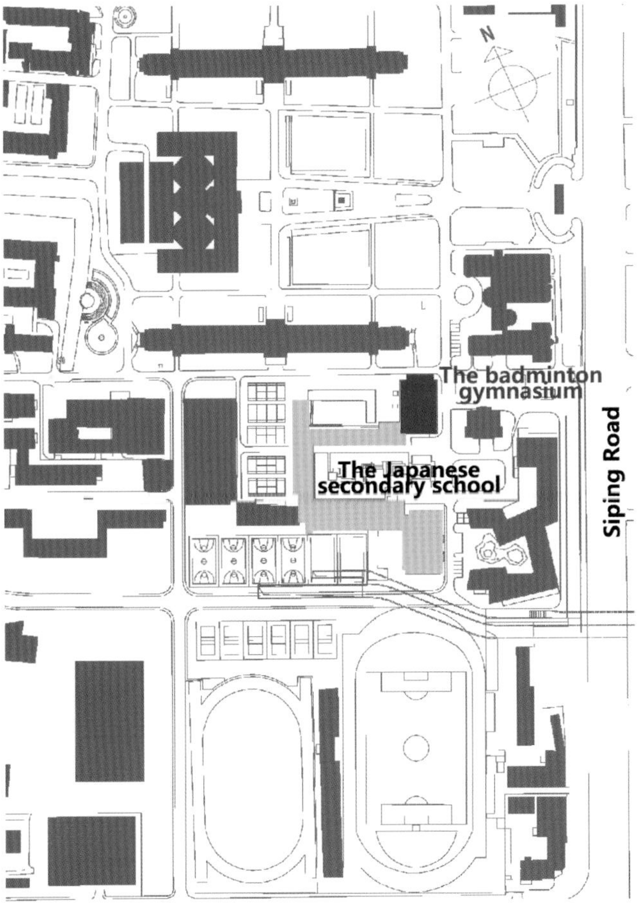

Figure 2
The badminton gymnasium at the campus

Figure 1
Site plan of the former Japanese secondary school

1. Introduction

The former Japanese secondary school that sits at the Siping Road Campus of Tongji University in the northern part of Shanghai was built in 1942 (Figure 1). Tongji University is now a world-famous academy focusing on civil engineering technology; the Siping Road Campus was founded in 1951. The badminton gymnasium lies near the main entrance of the campus; it is a low-key structure that has been neglected through time (Figure 2). However, it holds some hidden architectural "magic," for when one passes through the narrow pathway on the flank into the broad space created by the timber frame, they may suddenly experience a sense of "enlightenment" (Figure 3, page 6).

This study focuses on the badminton gymnasium, taking into account the following points:

1. The research on Shanghai's modern architectural history yields some positive highlights, most of which are concentrated in the International Settlement area and the French Concession,[1] while the research on Japanese architectural activities reveals less information because of the years of war—the Japanese army occupied Shanghai in November 1937, China won the Sino-Japanese war in August 1945; during the Japanese occupation, many Western architects left Shanghai and most Chinese architects retreated to inland China. Therefore, it is worth examining Japanese architectural activities in Shanghai in the 1940s. It is largely acknowledged that Japan played an important role in bringing the influences of Western approaches and technologies to Northern China in the 1930s and 1940s.

The study unveils significant findings concerning academic circles around the South Manchuria Railway Zones.[2] In comparison, less is informed about their architectural activities in Shanghai. Immigrants from Japan constituted the largest group of overseas migrants in Shanghai in the 1940s; the former Japanese secondary school was completed in 1942. The building is a clear and real part of Shanghai's architectural history and a direct outcome of Japanese immigrants forging their lives in Shanghai.

2. The Japanese Residents' League was endorsed by law in Shanghai in 1907, and governed Japanese who lived in either the International Settlement or the French Concession, also including the massive Japanese residences two miles outside of these designated areas. More than 70 percent of the pre-war financial budget for the Japanese Residents' League focused on education. The league's most important goal was the construction of eighteen primary and secondary schools.[3] For the purpose of this study, it is necessary to cite a key issue and select a completed school as a case study that sufficiently documents the journey of the architecture of Japanese immigrants.

3. The Japanese schools were continuously used for teaching until the 1990s when they were largely dismantled, with only a small number of them retained intact.[4] Tongji University's historic building cluster in its Siping Road campus was officially recognized and listed as a site of historic significance in 2005 by the Shanghai government and includes a badminton gymnasium which showcases certain special architectural features: a large-span design and a creative intent that was realized in the most feasible, logical way during then wartime conditions.

Kikuji Ishimoto designed several Japanese schools (for Japanese immigrants) in Shanghai in the 1940s, including the secondary school in Tongji University's Siping Road Campus. He is one of the more iconic Japanese modernist

Figure 3
Interior of the badminton gymnasium

Figure 4
The Japanese secondary school in 1942

architects that emerged during the 1920s Modern Movement. As Shanghai accepts many international architects from the concession, as well as famous Chinese architects educated by the West,[5] the degree of internationalization is broader in Shanghai than in Northern China. Modernist design by Japanese architects is an important part of China's international perspective.[6] The study on Ishimoto's practices in Shanghai has the potential to extend the modernistic influence beyond Northern China.

However, all archives about the former Japanese secondary school have long been lost because of the war, and interestingly, Ishimoto Architectural & Engineering (founded by Ishimoto) was also not aware that works such as the school still exist in Shanghai, which attached some challenges to the discussions with them. However, continuous communication with the firm created an increased interest on the subject and they graciously provided available historical photos from their archive for the study. The paper conducts in-depth research on the design of the school through the literature that was gathered on the school, as well as first-hand on-site surveying and mapping. It then analyzes and traces the development of modernism in timber structures (under the constraints of material scarcity during the war), and also provides a new clue for Shanghai's modern architecture pedigree to further and enrich subsequent studies on Japanese modernist architects who practiced in China during the war.

2. Overview of the Japanese Secondary School

2.1 Condition Restriction

The Japanese secondary school was built for boys, but not completed because of certain wartime rulings. It was

Figure 5
Professor Li Guohao introduces the general plan to experts from Eastern Germany in the 1950s. The former Japanese secondary school is on the left.

relocated to a new campus at Geemei Road (current Siping Road) in June 1940, and was completed in late 1942, attracting nearly 1,000 students. The campus area was 138,000 square meters; it had a 57,000-square-meter playground, three teaching buildings with fifteen ordinary classrooms and sixteen special classrooms, and one auditorium. The playground contained the badminton gymnasium, a judo court, kendo court, and a 400-meter racetrack. Compared with other Japanese schools in Shanghai, this school was a leader in both land occupation and building size (Figure 4, page 6).

At that time, the quality of Japanese education buildings built overseas usually far surpassed that of the schools in Japan itself, which makes the secondary school a favorable research subject. It is sad, however, to note that, unfortunately, actual education time at the school was rare, and the school was used more for political assembly and military or training purposes. Many students who went on for battles after they left the sanctuary of the school tragically died young.[7]

The financial assistance for building Japanese schools came partly from donations, bonds, and other income streams of the Japanese Residents' League in Shanghai. The rest was accumulated from the special allowance for school education provided by the Japanese government and Shanghai Municipal Council (SMC). Despite the availability of funds, construction of the school faced challenges. Construction materials were explicitly restricted even if the building standard of these schools far surpassed those of the domestic schools in Japan launched in the Sino-Japanese War because of the "License Rules for the Casting of Iron and Steel Workpieces" endorsed in 1937, which controlled the availability and use of steel and cement. Adding to that, construction activities unrelated to military supplies had also been stopped during that time. With the outbreak of the Pacific War in 1941, the shortage of construction materials took its toll on construction projects in Shanghai. During the Japanese occupation in Shanghai at that time, the Japanese controller adopted the same military supplies control method that was followed in Japan, and so reinforced-concrete was prohibited as a construction material for civil/public buildings without proper permission,[8] which led to the school inevitably being completed as a timber structure in 1942.

2.2 A Unified Character

The school's buildings that have been retained—namely making up the auditorium, teaching buildings, and badminton gymnasium—present a U-shape layout (Figure 5, page 6). The buildings face southwest and there is a sense of the coordinated order of a public space, which is created by its surroundings of cypress trees. As one end of a highly visible axis, the gymnasium is closely related to the opposite auditorium. There is a colonnade at the gymnasium's main entrance, and there are guide rails at the top and bottom of the frame to facilitate the easy push/pull of two large doors. A flagpole stands in the center of the public space, and so the landscape here is more commemorative. Both the building and site plan were undertaken by Ishimoto from 1940 to 1942. However, the original group of buildings has changed gradually since 2000. The auditorium has been renovated, with a glass foyer added to the exterior,[9] and the teaching building has been partially renovated into Tongji University Museum.[10] Located at the end of the cluster, the badminton gymnasium is the only original structure untouched by modern updates. Apart from routine maintenance, painting, and

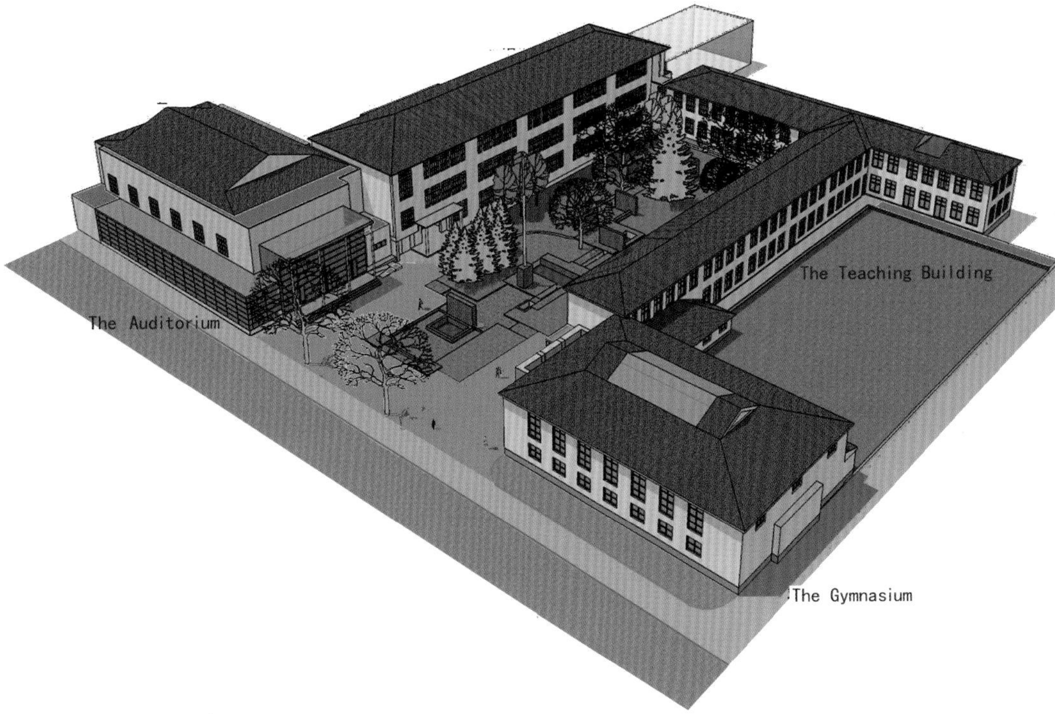

Figure 6
Cooperative education complex

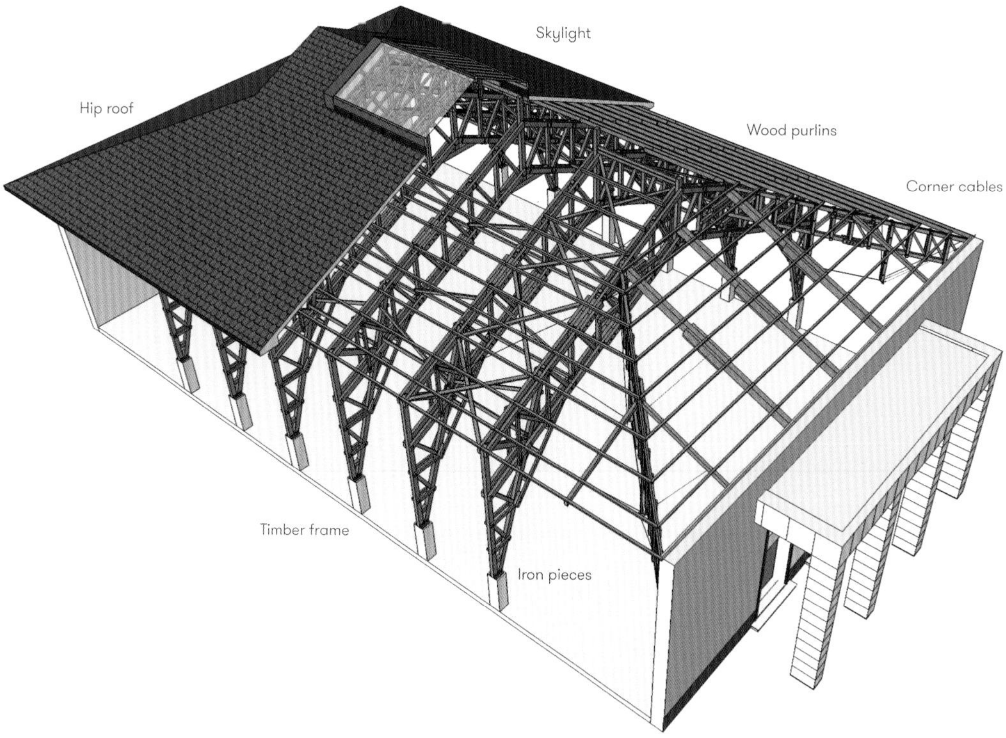

Figure 7
Axonometric section of badminton gymnasium

ensuring that the waterproofing holds up, there have been no changes to the functions or layout of the gymnasium, enabling it to fully reflect the architect's intentions (Figure 6, page 7).

Traditional Japanese roofs can be divided into four types: gable roof, hip roof, gable-and-hip roof, and multi-angle roof. According to a general survey of the roof types of important historical and cultural properties in Japan, the proportion of gable-and-hip roof that was used in buildings was relatively high, covering many types of structures, such as farmhouses, tearooms, and shrines, unofficially turning this roof typology into a symbol of Japanese tradition. Basing the study's deduction on the time's strict economic situation, it is observed that Ishimoto adopted the school's structural selection reasonably. The teaching building was built with masonry, employing a Howe timber truss for the hip roof; the auditorium was designed with a steel-and-wood structure to accommodate its gable-and-hip roof; and the badminton gymnasium uses a larch portal frame, mainly for a gable-and-hip roof, which was an ideal solution for large-span constructions, given its aesthetic significance. By analyzing the distributions of strengths together, Ishimoto was able to give a coherent picture of the types of timber structures through a unified character.

2.3 A Traditional Portal Frame with Stability and Elegance

The badminton gymnasium was positioned at the end of the U-shaped cluster, and connected with the teaching building on one side. It had a floor area of about 800 square meters and is 21.4 meters wide and 37.2 meters long. It was a single-story building that featured a gable-and-hip roof, a glass skylight in the ridge, and a row of auxiliary rooms on the flank (Figure 7). The badminton gymnasium's main court was 20.6 by 32.4 meters. (After April

Figure 8
The Golden Ratio of the portal frame

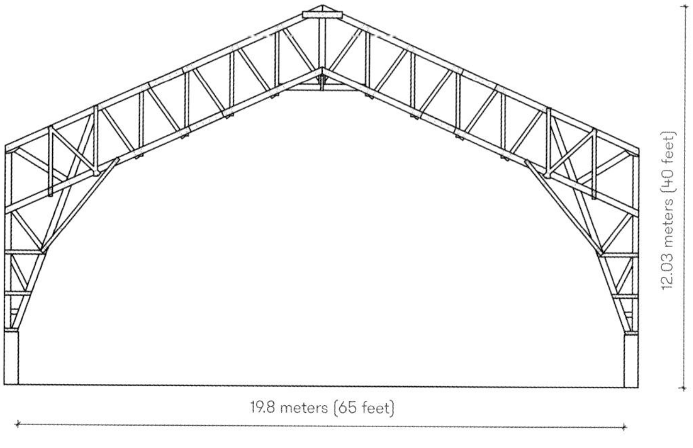

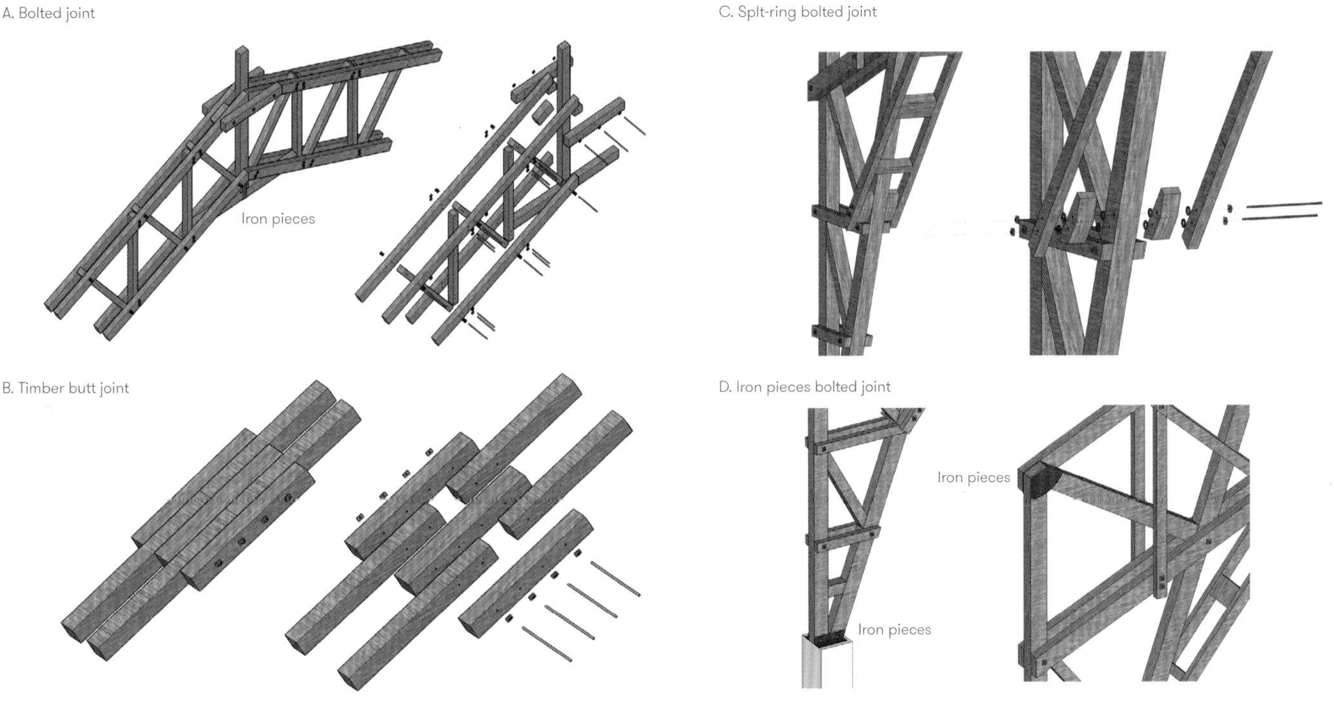

Figure 9
Joints analysis

1921, the use of the metric system was encouraged in Japan by the Measuring Correction Act. However, it was adopted in architectural design only after World War II—and done so mainly because of its deep-rooted usage in the society. From the beginning, Ishimoto used the imperial system, which made it easier for traditional craft processing in Shanghai, hence all data from the survey is accorded to imperial units.)

Accordingly, the portal frame which the badminton gymnasium used was for a single-span or multi-span structural system composed of a roof truss and columns. The beam and column were rigidly connected, and the column was hinged with the foundation. In the interior, the use of reinforcing plates and rivets connected the beam and frame column, forming the prominent characteristics of the portal frame: large space, beam column integration, less component types, and clear force transmission. The six timber portal frames undertook the main load of the roof; the roof truss and the column constituted the single-span system, in which beams were rigidly connected with columns by bracings, and the pillars finally transmitted the force to the base. Even if the portal frame belongs to a traditional way of construction, it's use in the badminton gymnasium reveals innovations that course with many others in the historical river of modern architecture.

In 1956, Ludwig Mies van der Rohe adeptly used the exposed portal frame in Crown Hall at Illinois Institute of Technology (IIT), which challenged the steel structural span. And although the badminton gymnasium featured the similar idea of a portal frame, the form of the gymnasium varied significantly, due to a shortage of materials at the time of construction. The gymnasium determined the architectural aesthetics, structural engineering, and economic strategies as a whole. It had to meet the need of a specific space in a low cost, with simple timber as building material, as well as be executed as a clear form. The larch portal frame was high in the middle and low on both sides, meeting the "use" requirements of the large-span in the center of the ground very well. The eave height of the whole truss frame was 7.5 meters (22 feet and 6 inches); the distance from the center top of the frame to the ground was 12.03 meters (40 feet); and the span was 19.8 meters (65 feet). The height-span ratio was 0.612, near the Golden Ratio proportion that has been heralded as the most classic scale of balance for many centuries (Figure 8, page 8). Japanese architectural design has always had a good reputation globally, in terms of technical aspects and aesthetic appeal. Based on Ishimoto's design and concept process, it is deduced that that the elegant structural form of the gymnasium is consistent with the Golden Ratio to pique visual perception.

Should there be any strong wind loads or earthquakes, the lateral displacement of the frame would be the main cause of deformation. Therefore, to guarantee lateral rigidity, the gymnasium was designed with a deeply embedded square-base reinforced-concrete foundation. Five groups of continuous wooden members were added between the six timber portal frames, thus strengthening the overall rigidity of the architectural structure. In addition, connecting wooden pieces were added between the two-truss portal frames. Instability was sometimes partially also related to the design of joints, and so the frame members of the structure of the badminton gymnasium were connected by galvanized bolts with a diameter of 15 millimeters, which were supported by metallic shims with a diameter of 50 millimeters. In order to avoid splitting in the keyways, small wooden members were used in some parts to enlarge the section to resist the twisting of the timber parts

Figure 10
Comparison between truss corner of teaching building (above) and badminton gymnasium (below)

(Figure 9—jointing A and B, page 9); the bolts in the widest position of the diagonal bracing of the frame were connected by using metallic rings to strengthen the effect—that is, using the ring connections in the wooden structure, which was a special technique in early timber buildings (Figure 9—jointing C, page 9). The badminton gymnasium only used some steel parts to overcome large bending moments to increase the rigidity of the truss (Figure 9—jointing D, page 9). The architect avoided a complex design that would have been difficult to construct by taking into consideration both stability and the time's economic conditions.

2.4 An Innovative Cable Supported Structure

The rationality, cost, and technical stability of the structure complement each other. Through the unity of force and beauty, the badminton gymnasium conveys the design strategy and emotion that Ishimoto wanted to express. The six timber portal frames form the construction of the long side of the gable-and-hip roof. So then, in such a design situation, how would the short-side roof-ridge be finished?

Usually, the construction of a gable roof or a hip roof features the use of a triangular truss at the corners, which is enclosed in a suspended ceiling; a good example is the design of the top corner of the hip roof of the teaching building of the school. The advantage is the perfect stability of the triangle, but the disadvantage is the significant consumption of materials and the waste of interior height. So, instead, the badminton gymnasium finds an innovative way that achieves results. The entire structure is exposed and demonstrates a power of angle joints design (Figure 10). The downturned roof-ridge in the hall makes use of a cable supported structure, where "cable" refers to the stay

Figure 11
Additional members among portal frames

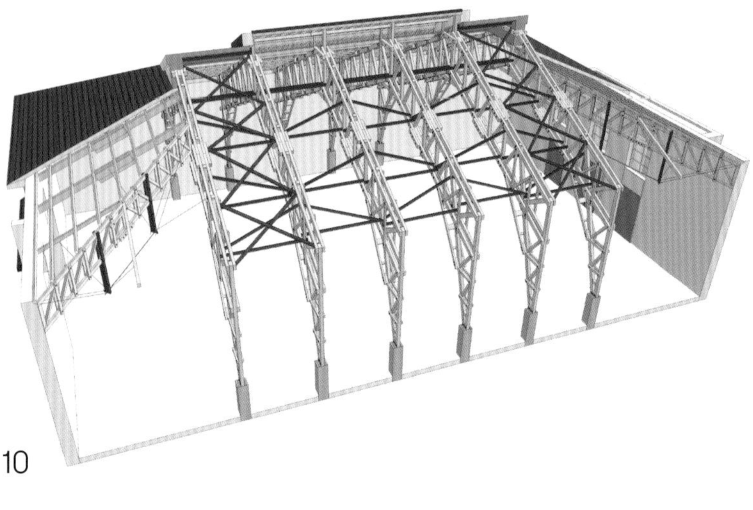

Figure 12
Badminton gymnasium plan and line of sight analysis

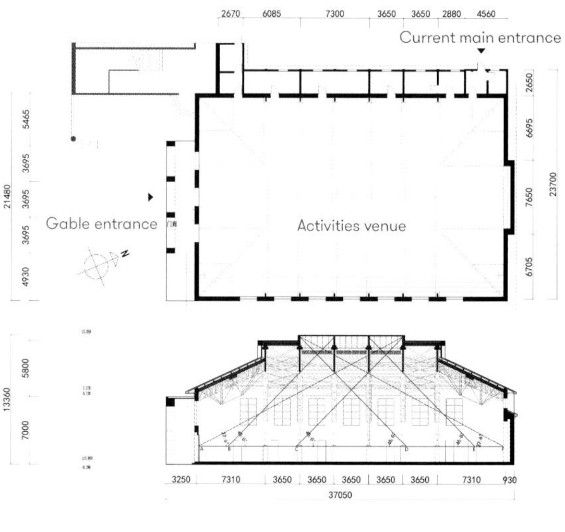

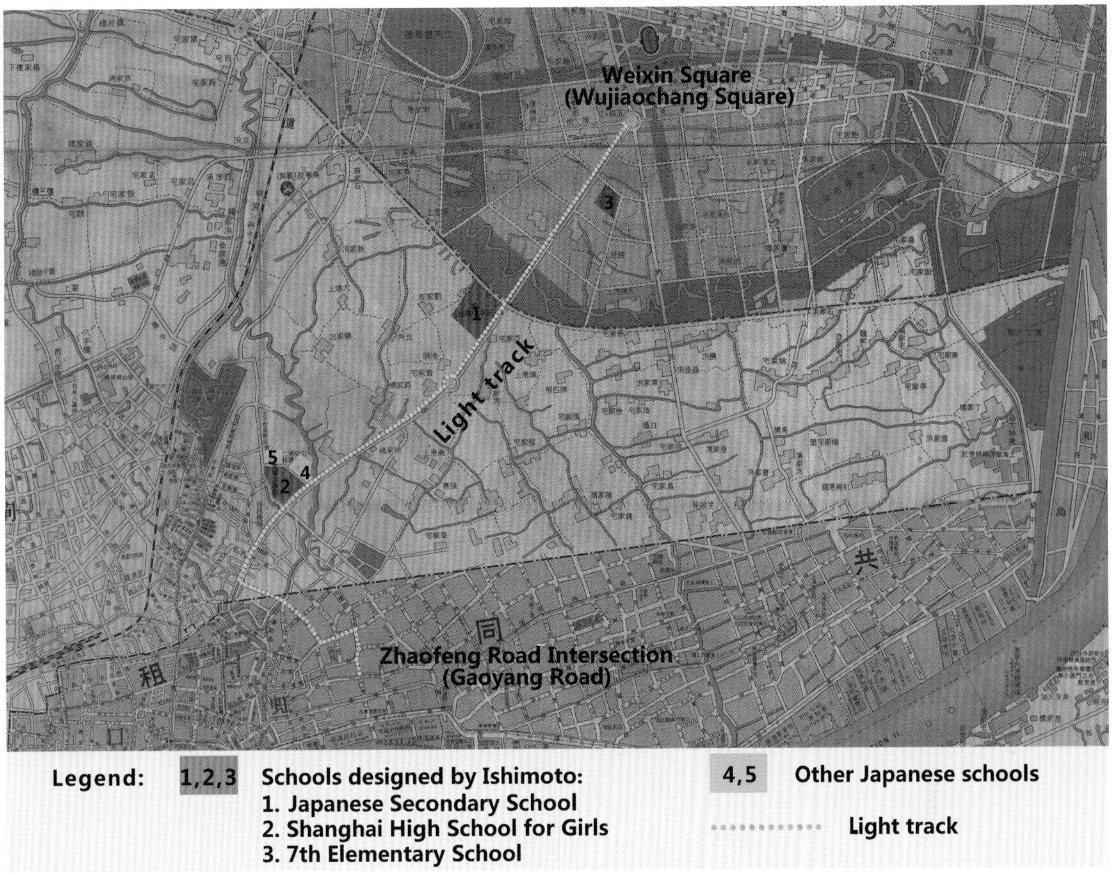

Figure 13
The light rail from 1939 to 1944 connecting Hongkew district with Wujiaochang Square

bracing at the bottom of the structure, and "supported" refers to the pressure bar at the center of the structure.[11] The specific form is used at the angle part of the badminton gymnasium, where one 45-degree inclined wooden beam is in symmetrical arrangement with two compression bars and nine steel bracing cables, which are anchored at the end of the timber frame (Figure 11, page 10). The lower bracing cable is tightened, reducing the external thrust of the inclined beam to the support base. And with this, structural innovation is formed without any new materials. This design provided the building with a light, but strong system, and with that, also achieved the improvement of construction efficiency, as well as utilization. The gymnasium benefited from Ishimoto's full understanding and skillful use of stress balance and force transmission.

2.5 The Light for a Panoramic Experience

The gymnasium is fitted with vertical windows at the lateral sides, small windows at the gable, and a glass skylight in the ridge. Natural light is a cheap (and even free) source that enables another structural landscape. The ridge's daylighting system was designed strictly, with a skylight that extends lengthwise, spanning three portal truss frames. It compensated the modest daylighting from the lateral windows and improved the uniformity of daylighting. Incident rays are shaded by the portal frame and become gentler with the reduced intensity, helping to avoid glare. In the use and appreciation (with regards to space, structure, and light flow) of the badminton gymnasium, both 27- and 45-degree angles hold much significance, making it possible to obtain a compact panoramic experience from either the gable wall entrance or the main entrance (Figure 12, page 10). The badminton gymnasium has exquisite proportions and it may be inferred that Ishimoto was skilled at both classical and modern architectural design methods.

Under the limited economic and technical resources, Ishimoto depicts space modeling through reasonable design, and makes the structure itself more distinctive, maximizing that aspect. Structure selection is particularly prominent in large spaces with pure functions, such as a church, warehouse, or gymnasium. These spaces are both commemorative and functional under certain light and shadow.

3. Modernist Architect Kikuji Ishimoto (1894–1963) in Shanghai

The original archives of the former Japanese secondary school were totally lost owing to the war. The study's research process began with obtaining the interview with Ishimoto, recorded by Professor Lu Bingjie, an expert in the field of architecture history in the College of Architecture and Urban Planning at Tongji University. In the early 1980s, Professor Lu met Professor Kunio Maekawa (1905–1986) when he was a visiting scholar at The University of Tokyo, from whom he learnt that Ishimoto, a professor at The University of Tokyo, was in charge of building the Japanese secondary school in Shanghai.

3.1 History Speaks

A light rail starts from the intersection of Tangshan Road and Zhaofeng Road (Gaoyang Road), which is densely populated and close to the Huangpu River wharf. Other public transportation systems are easily connected to the site. The track crosses the international settlement and goes north along Weixin Road (previously Geemei Road, then Songjing Road, and later Siping Road) to Weixin Square (Wujiaochang Square) in Greater Shanghai, extending a total length of about 7 kilometers (Figure 13, page 11). (It may be speculated that the subgrade of the road at that time was treated to meet the needs of light rail operation.) This light rail is built by Shanghai Hengchan Co., Ltd. (上海恒产股份有限公司/恒产株式会社), a Japanese-funded company with a political association with the Japanese colonial government and China's (then) "puppet" government. In 1938, Shanghai Hengchan drafts out the Greater Shanghai Construction Project (上海都市建设计划图); Ishimoto's work is closely related to Hengchan's development.

There are five Japanese schools along the track line, which have been specially designed for migrant students. Ishimoto designs three of them, including the former Japanese secondary school. The areas around the school are collectively named as the first residential district, while the secondary school lies close to the Greater Shanghai planned boundary for the new town.

Maekawa also designs many high-quality residences in the new town. A few of them still exist today in the Air Force's courtyard, according to Liu Gang's research. The light rail gets dismantled in 1944 due to the need for steel, which shows that the war was tremendously serious, and had a significant impact.

3.2 Ishimoto's Schools and Later Years

It can be confirmed that Shanghai High School for Girls and the Japanese 7th Elementary School in Jiangwan District, Shanghai, were both designed by Ishimoto in 1942 and 1941, respectively, but the former Japanese secondary school was the first one to be finished. The Japanese 7th Elementary School was a modern building cluster, with a similar timber portal frame built in the gymnasium. Comparing historical photos of the Japanese 7th Elementary School gymnasium with the current badminton gymnasium of the Japanese secondary school, it can be seen that that there is some consistency in structural proportions, such as in the roof skylight and the three point-type windows at the gable. This provides additional evidence in the textual research that a standard design system could have been created by Ishimoto, providing technical, robust, and repeatable results (Figure 14). Ishimoto executed at least three teaching buildings in Hongkew District and Yangpu District of Greater Shanghai from 1940 to 1942, however, only the site of the former Japanese secondary school is still retained today.

The Japanese Secessionist Architects Organization (Bunri-ha) is generally considered the first avant-garde modernist architectural movement in Japan, which begun in 1920. Ishimoto was one of the founding members of the organization. The members of Bunri-ha subsequently followed two different routes: one pursuing the structural technology school, and the other pursuing the aesthetic school. Ishimoto, who followed both, had studied at Tokyo Imperial University (The University of Tokyo), taking modules on structural mechanics and structural principles, along with arts training. The traditional wooden structure—as one of the major characteristics of Japanese buildings, which results partly from the frequent earthquakes in the region—has a vital impact on Japanese architects' vocational education.[12] Ishimoto was the first Japanese architect to ever follow Walter Gropius at Bauhaus-Universität Weimar, with whom he stayed in contact for a long time, in a way having direct contact with European modernism; this, later, naturally aligned him with Bauhaus's and Japanese philosophy. The young architect emerged vividly in a changing world with

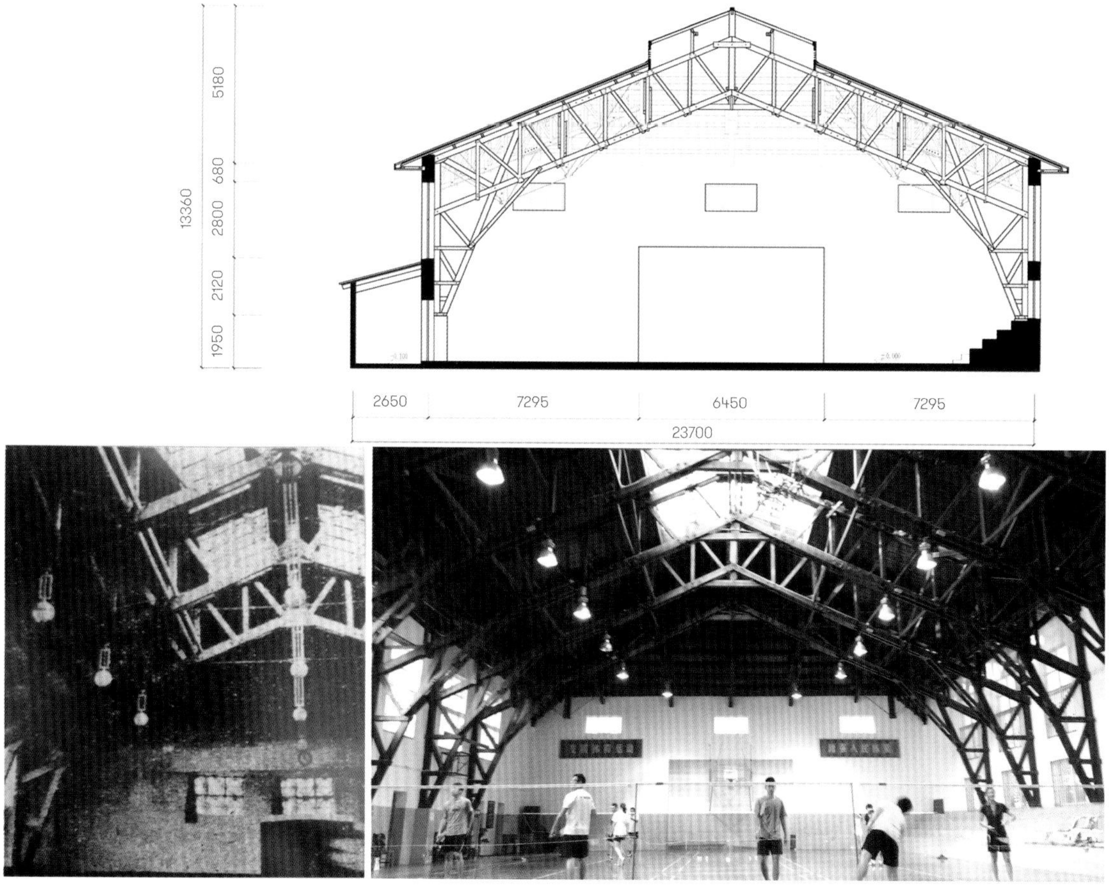

Figure 14
Comparison of the Japanese 7th Elementary School gymnasium (left) and Tongji University Siping Road Campus's badminton gymnasium (right)

Figure 15
Kikuji Ishimoto Studio in Shanghai with the Japanese 7th Elementary School

works which could also have been influenced by his wife, Mrs. Ishimoto, who was a professor in the Fine Arts Department at Nihon University, advancing the cause of modern art design education.[13]

After returning to Japan, Ishimoto engaged in his architectural activities through noted Takenaka Corporation and Shimizu Corporation (清水组).[14] In 1927, he completed the Tokyo Asahi Shinbun building, which was a significant accomplishment. Today, the building is authorized as a cultural property under the national protection law. Unofficially, and unintentionally, taking on the role as a pioneer in Japanese modernism, Ishimoto established Kataoka & Ishimoto Architectural Planning Company in 1931, when young Maekawa was still learning at Le Corbusier's atelier in Paris. When Sino-Japanese hostilities broke out in 1937, Ishimoto received many orders for military facilities and buildings. As the ravages of war began to extend to Japan, orders for normal structures or buildings for civilian uses became almost non-existent. In response, the development toward the overseas colonies and occupied territory became the main projects of Japanese architects at that time. Ishimoto set up Ishimoto-Kawai Architectural Studio in Hsinking (Changchun) in 1938; the studio simultaneously expanded a branch into Shanghai with multiple projects, including temporary army dormitories and migrant schools. The architect was busy with projects in Japan, Hsinking, and Shanghai, which continued till the defeat of Japan in 1945.[15] Despite conditions of extreme economic difficulties, Ishimoto's works conveyed the characteristics of the modern structural technical school, later becoming the epitome of the times.

The former Japanese secondary school has a complete form. The truss gable roof benefits from good heat insulation and rain-proofing, which was suitable for Shanghai's climate and technical conditions at that time. Ishimoto used masonry and a steel-wood-timber portal frame to form a highly unified prototype. Modern architecture creates a flat top and horizontal windows in different cultures and different regions, achieving different functions. The flat top seems to be the identity recognized by the public. Old photos reveal that modernist architects attempted to deliberately weaken the gable roof to express a smooth geometry. According to photos of a school in Shanghai that existed around that time—provided by Ishimoto Architectural & Engineering Firm (Figure 15)—it can be seen that the school had a modernist media image rather than a traditional building one. Respectively, the badminton gymnasium at Siping Road campus presents two envelopes: its façade is very simple, presenting the colonnade, window, and roof characteristics. On the other hand, people will enjoy the extremely expressive timber portal frame on entering the building. It can be seen that modernist architecture removes all the ornaments and takes structure-form as the core, with an organic reasoning and point, fundamentally to the origin of space—which was perhaps an emergency response to the high-pressure life during the war.

Unfortunately, there is a lack of information on the construction processes of the Japanese 7th Elementary School and the former Japanese secondary school designed by Ishimoto. It can be deduced that the construction team was Shiraido Michi Corporation (白井道上组), and that the construction of the former Japanese secondary school would have been completed by a Japanese company. At that time, Japanese architects teamed with construction factories so that communication would be more convenient and the traditional wooden structure method could be easily carried out. Mechanization was very low, requiring more manual operation during those hard times.

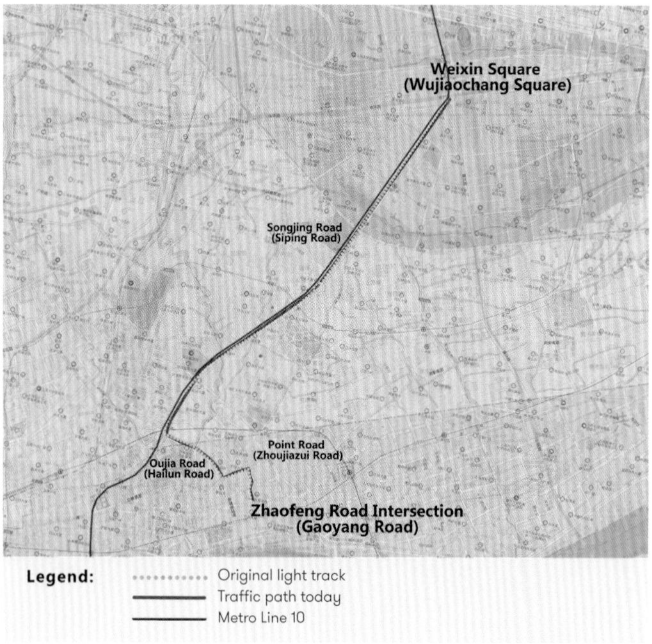

Figure 16
Today's traffic line coincides with the demolished light rail line built by the Japanese in the 1940s

Figure 17
A Sino-Japanese exchange activity in 1983

4. Conclusion

Japanese modern architecture began to lay its foundation in the 1920s. Noted Japanese architects brought this style to Shanghai, forging the path for Japanese modern architecture to become one of the most important schools of modernism in the metropolis. By analyzing the construction of the timber portal frame of the badminton gymnasium on Siping Road Campus and tracing the historical role of modernism, it can be inferred that Japanese modernist architects paid attention to materials, structure, and construction technology, and concentrated on the accumulation of aesthetic perception. Aesthetic idea and suitable technology were the necessary premise for Japanese architecture to reach a leading international level after World War II. Time elapses and timber heritage transcending national boundaries was an indispensable part of the evolution of modernism.[16] In addition to the study of modernism style, it is also quite necessary to consider the construction nodes and cable supporting system. These fully reflect the traditional way of Japanese wooden structures being constructed at a certain stage; it is an important carrier of emotive memory.

As time goes by, the condition of the badminton gymnasium ages and the historic building needs regular maintenance. The school's journey from Hongkew to Wujiaochang plays an important role in analyzing the influence of Japanese colonists on the modern urban planning of Shanghai.

The urban fabric has changed and the light rail path on the ground has merged, due to the redevelopment of the plot, but it is still used as a main traffic road, even including an overlap with Metro Line 10, which indicates that the development along the line has historical inheritance (Figure 16). The colonial landscape on the ground has also been replaced totally by the modern public service facilities of international metropolises.

A few details can be concluded of the badminton gymnasium of the school that was active years ago (Figure 17). Being a dynamic sports venue for students, and, occasionally, an exciting assembly hall for international experts (Figure 18, page 15), this masterpiece demonstrates the flexibility and potential of a large-span timber building on the campus. Japanese modernist architects used wooden structures to create education complexes, where the style no longer pursued a modernist one, but conformed to the political, economic, and cultural context of modern architecture at a particular time. These buildings are worthy of attention as Asia's modernism heritage.

When we fully understand such significant stories in history, there will be more comprehensive and objective evidence that can be collected, even if this evidence is attached to time ranges where there were times of conflict between countries. When we are able to understand mutual opinions, academic exchanges will naturally expand in the future.

Acknowledgments

The authors would like to acknowledge the financial support of the National Natural Science Foundation of China (NSFC: 51978471).

Figure 18
An international assembly in 2019

Notes

1. Lu Hanchao, *Beyond the Neon Lights: Everyday Shanghai in the Early Twentieth Century* (San Francisco: University of California Press, 2004), 80.
2. Xu Subin, *Japanese Studies on Chinese Cities and Architecture* (Beijing: China Water Power Press, 1999), 91–93.
3. Wu Jianxi, "The Japanese Residents' Association and Shanghai Imigrant School," *Historical Review* (Apr. 1994): 23–24.
4. Shanghai Archives, May 21, 1946. The National Government: Property Directory of the First, Seventh Japanese Primary Schools Collected in SMA. File no. Q235-2-4834.
5. H. Goto-Shibata, *Japan and Britain in Shanghai, 1925–31* (London: Palgrave Macmillan, 1995), 30.
6. Takatsuna Hirofum, *The Social History of Overseas Japanese in Modern Shanghai*, trans. Chen Zu'en (Shanghai: Shanghai People's Publishing House, 2014), 8.
7. Li Minxun, *Centennial Annals of Tongji University* (Shanghai: Tongji University Press, 2007), 12–13.
8. Akira Koshizawa, *The Capital Planning of Puppet Manchuria* (Beijing: Social Sciences Literature Press, 2011), 22.
9. Zuo Yan, "Highlighting the Historical Charm of Architecture: The Transformation of the Auditorium of Tongji University," *Times Architecture*, no. 98 (Apr. 2001): 78–83.
10. Xie Zhenyu, "The Excavation and Promotion of Value — The Design Experience of the Renovation of Tongji '129' Teaching Building into Tongji University Museum," *Times Architecture*, no. 150 (Feb. 2014): 88–93.
11. Chen Zhihua, "Cable Supported Structure and Classification," *Industrial Building*, no. 311 (Aug. 2010): 76–83.
12. Takeshi Asakawa and Toshihiko Kouno, "Long-span Wooden Structural Beams Assembled with Four-meter-long Timbers Using Japanese Traditional Connections," IABSE Symposium Report, November 2010, pages 228–234.
13. Yao Tsun-Hsiung, Sun Chu-Yu, and Lin Pin-Chang, "Modern Design in Taiwan: The Japanese Period, 1895–1945," *Massachusetts Institute of Technology Design Issues*, vol. 29, no. 3 (2013): 38–51.
14. Jonathan M, *Maekawa Kunio and the Emergence of Japanese Modernism* (Oakland: University of California Press, Reynolds, Berkeley and Los Angeles, 2001), 10–14.
15. Kikuji Ishimoto, "Japanese 7th Elementary School," *Japanese Architect*, no. 30 (Jan. 1942): 65–66.
16. Shanghai Municipal People's Government, Regulations of Shanghai Municipality on the Protection of the Areas with Historical Cultural Features and the Excellent Historical Buildings, 2005.

Figure Credits

Figure 1: The site plan of the former Japanese secondary school (authors' drawing).
Figure 2: The badminton gymnasium at the campus (authors' photo).
Figure 3: Interior of the badminton gym (© Peng Nu).
Figure 4: The Japanese secondary school in 1942 (Lu Minxun, *Tongji Lao Zhao Pian* [*Tongji Old Photos*], Expanded Edition, Shanghai, China: Tongji Daxue Chubanshe [Tongji University Press], 2007, 17; reproduced with permission).
Figure 5: Professor Li Guohao introduces the general plan to experts from Eastern Germany in the 1950s. The former Japanese secondary school is on the left (Lu Minxun, *Tongji Lao Zhao Pian* [*Tongji Old Photos*], Expanded Edition, Shanghai, China: Tongji Daxue Chubanshe [Tongji University Press], 2007, 205; reproduced with permission).
Figure 6: Cooperative education complex (Drawn by Xie Zhenyu).
Figure 7: Axonometric section of the badminton gymnasium (authors' drawing).
Figure 8: The Golden Ratio of the portal frame (authors' drawing).
Figure 9: Joints analysis (authors' drawing).
Figure 10: Comparison between truss corner of teaching building (above) and badminton gymnasium corner cable (below) (authors' photos).
Figure 11: Additional members among portal frames (authors' drawing).
Figure 12: Badminton gymnasium plan and line of sight analysis (authors' drawing).
Figure 13: The light track from 1939 to 1944, connecting Hongkew district with Wujiaochang Square (author's drawing based on The New Map of Great Shanghai [1943], Maps of China, Late Qing Dynasty-1949, The Hong Kong University of Science and Technology Library, Call no. G7824.S2 1943 .S84; reproduced with permission).
Figure 14: Comparison of the Japanese 7th Elementary School gymnasium (left) and Tongji University Siping Road Campus's badminton gymnasium (right) (authors' drawing; photo courtesy of Ishimoto Architectural & Engineering Firm).
Figure 15: Kikuji Ishimoto Studio in Shanghai with the Japanese 7th Elementary School (photo courtesy of Ishimoto Architectural & Engineering Firm).
Figure 16: Today's traffic line coincides with the demolished light rail line built by the Japanese in the 1940s (author's map overlay of Zhaofeng Road and Tangshan Road intersection; map sources: Baidu Maps and The New Map of Great Shanghai [1943], Maps of China, Late Qing Dynasty-1949, The Hong Kong University of Science and Technology Library, Call no. G7824.S2 1943 .S84; reproduced with permission).
Figure 17: Sino-Japanese exchange activity in 1983 (photo courtesy of Tongji University Physical Education Department).
Figure 18: An international assembly in 2019 (authors' photo).

Prescriptive Urban Greening Strategies for a Saturated Megacity: Reflections on Kolkata, India

Souporni PAUL, Jadavpur University, India
Suchandra BARDHAN, Jadavpur University, India

Abstract

Urban growth in middle-income nations like India usually happens beyond the infrastructural and environmental capacity a city can sustain, leading to loss of valuable natural resources. Most Indian cities suffer from congestion, poor environmental conditions, and a shortage of green areas. Urban green space (UGS) is fundamental to a city because of its ecological, social, economic, and health benefits. In conjunction with conventional urban planning policies, management tools, and regulatory frameworks, there is a necessity for adopting new urban greening strategies that can profoundly improve unhealthy living conditions. This paper studies the spatial distribution of UGS and discusses specific greening strategies in the Indian city of Kolkata, at its smallest administrative unit, referred to as "wards." The recommended strategies based on the landscape ecological approach and practical implementation methods derive from a realistic assessment of opportunities and barriers that can help to reinforce green coverage, from the neighborhood to the city level.

Author Information
Souporni PAUL: souporni@gmail.com, ORCID ID: 0000-0002-4813-6199
Suchandra BARDHAN: suchandrab@gmail.com

Keywords

Urban green space (UGS), green area distribution, greening strategies, urban greening.

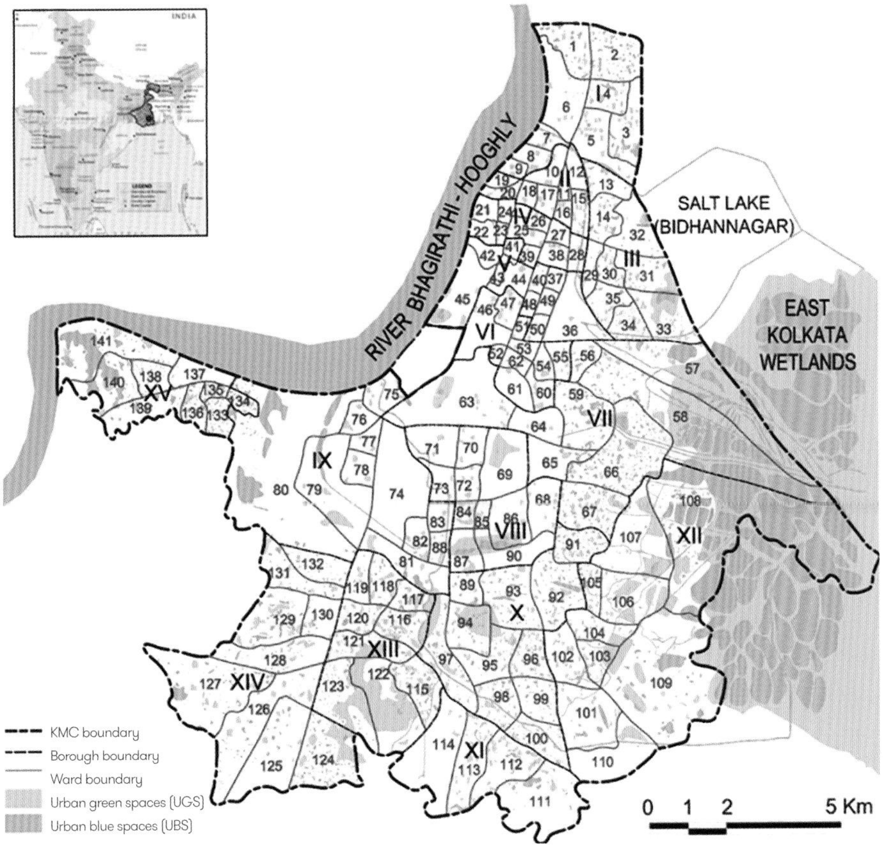

Figure 1
Map of Kolkata showing the spatial distribution of urban green spaces and wetlands in 2020

1. Introduction

Green space is broadly defined as "open, undeveloped land with natural vegetation, such as parks, forests, playgrounds, and river corridors."[1] Urban green spaces (UGS) are public and private open spaces with vegetation in urban areas, directly or indirectly available to the city's inhabitants.[2] In other words, they are the city's visual and accessible green areas consisting fundamentally of permeable surfaces covered with soil or vegetation.[3] They contribute to the city's ecological, social, and economic benefits, while making it resilient to unprecedented future challenges like climate change, loss of biodiversity, stormwater management, urban heat island mitigation, and disruption of ecosystem services.[4, 5]

Ever since the garden city concept was advocated by urban planner Ebenezer Howard in England, and the urban park movement during the nineteenth century was established in the United Sates by landscape architect Frederick Law Olmsted, UGS has become a crucial part of the urban environment. A city can be livable and environmentally sustainable when there is a proportionate share of green spaces and built-up areas to satisfy all the social, environmental, and recreational needs of the community.[6, 7] Providing access for all sections of the society to safe, inclusive, and accessible, green and public spaces in cities has also been recommended in the UN Sustainable Development Goal 11.7.[8] For example, as a city grows or as the population rises, there is often a need to continuously upgrade and expand infrastructures such as roads, sewers, and public utilities. Similarly, it is also necessary to upgrade and expand its green infrastructure, such as green spaces and water bodies, which form the ecological backbone of the city's environmental and economic sustainability. Cities in middle-income nations like India are fast losing their natural areas due to the rapid pace of urbanization and their increasing population.[9] Accelerated development results in the urban landscape becoming more fragmented, with disrupted ecosystem services, poor living standards, and limited access to safe green spaces for the residents.

This article studies the spatial distribution of UGS in the Indian city of Kolkata (formerly Calcutta), the state-capital of West Bengal. With a population density of around 24,760 per square kilometer,[10] Kolkata is a growing megacity which faces rising pressures on its existing natural resources, given its ever-increasing population, urban sprawl, inadequate infrastructure, and poor governance.[11, 12]

Kolkata is a city with a rich natural heritage. Located in the floodplains of the lower Gangetic delta, the city prospers with various naturally complex ecological systems, such as the East Kolkata Wetlands, River Bhagirathi-Hooghly, River Adi Ganga, and an efficient canal system alongside innumerable anthropogenic landscape reserves like national lakes, urban parks, and public and private gardens. However, on the map of Kolkata, the physical environment is barely visible in the dense urban fabric; they remain as discontinuous fragments of the original ecosystems. Major encroachment on the eastern periphery of the wetlands for real estate has had a drastic influence on land-use patterns and resource management. Several studies show that with the drastic increase in urban settlements, there is a steady decline in vegetation patches, tree coverage, and wetlands,[13, 14, 15] and the urban forest cover—the best sink for carbon dioxide and suspended dust particles—and biodiversity reserve has become almost non-existent.[16] Kolkata's tree cover fell from 23.4 percent to 7.3 percent over twenty years,[17] and urban and neighborhood parks, mainly utilized and accessed by the local people for their recreational needs, cover only 5.5 percent of the total study area.[18] This research aims to quantify and analyze the proportion of UGS at the municipal ward (the smallest administrative unit) level and formulate strategies for improving the same concerning different categories of wards. Urban greening strategies are developed in terms of short-term and long-term actions for qualitative and quantitative promotions of green areas in Kolkata. These locally derived and locally appropriate strategies include a cost-effective and easy methodology to procure an accurate database, identify the gap, and bridge this gap by practical implementation methods involving public participation in an ecologically sustainable approach. The methodology can be applied to any Indian city to reorientate its current development pathway toward a sustainable trajectory. However, they need to be aligned with other sectors like solid waste management, water and sanitation, transportation, and finally, ecosystem and biodiversity management, to achieve a holistic outcome in urban regeneration.

2. Materials and Methodology

The study area consists of the 144 wards of the Kolkata Municipal Corporation (KMC), which are grouped into sixteen boroughs (administrative blocks). The paper elaborates on the process of urban greening in a four-step integrated framework comprising the following: i) a detailed assessment of existing status; ii) identification of zonal categories based on the distribution of green spaces; iii) identification of the barriers; and iv) strategy recommendations for each zone.

In the first phase of the study, the primary objective was to conduct a built open space relationship in the city to gain a general overview of the cityscape. The assessment is based on the review of existing literature and analysis of secondary data from various sources, such as maps and reports available from KMC and other government agencies. Data was retrieved (extracted) from the parks of Kolkata, the Center for Contemporary Communication, Google Earth, and KMC ward maps.[19] The Kolkata map (Figure 1, page 17) was digitized in AutoCAD 2018 to get the exact extent and accurate numerical value of each UGS at year 2020. This was followed by preparing a second map (Figure 1, page 17) as an overlay showing the ward-wise percentage distribution of UGS. These helped to identify the distribution of green spaces in the city and wards that fare low in terms of available green areas, and which need immediate attention in terms of planning strategies. A pragmatic approach ranging from inserting plantable spaces in the smallest residential unit, to a broader transformation at the regional level involving administrative and public participation is recommended.

3. Results and Discussions

3.1. A Detailed Assessment of the Existing Status

Kolkata was established as a port city during the British rule on the eastern bank of the Bhagirathi-Hooghly River, merging three villages, Gobindapur, Kalikata, and Sutanuti. Much of the city was originally a vast wetland, particularly on the eastern periphery, known as East Kolkata Wetlands, which has been a Ramsar site—a wetland site designated to be of international importance under the Ramsar Convention—since 2002. Since there was no possibility of expansion toward the west, due to the river, Kolkata progressively expanded toward the east, reclaiming the wetlands. The expansion was incited after the independence of India to accommodate a massive population influx from neighboring states and countries. Due to this unplanned and unexpected densification, the city got overcrowded with insufficient urban facilities, inefficient and inequitable infrastructure, and unsustainable practices, leading to environmental deterioration.[20]

Presently, Kolkata is a sprawling urban agglomeration revealing a predominantly residential land-use pattern with an uneven distribution of UGS (Figure 1, page 17). The entire north and most of central Kolkata is dominated by residential and commercial land-use and has a higher population density than the remaining parts of the city. The only significant portion of green space around central Kolkata is Maidan. This means that residents living in apartments, ownership houses, and slums have little or no opportunities to access green spaces. Spatially, the city's southern, eastern, and western peripheries have a substantial portion of open areas. These are relatively newer sectors of the city that have been incorporated from adjacent non-built-up areas and, therefore, designed according to efficient bylaws for open spaces. Some of the southern and eastern peripheries have significant proportions of arable lands within them. This unequal distribution of UGS affords an advantage to the western and southern residents over their northern counterparts in access, recreation, and contact with nature. The calculated UGS is 7.93 percent of the total urban area; the standard recommendation is 14 to 16 percent of the total urban area.[21] Kolkata is a dense, compact city with limited interstitial spaces for greenery. It can be challenging to find a large area for new green spaces and attention must be given to more minor interventions and multi-beneficial connections, and green infrastructure.

3.2 Identification of Zonal Categories Based on the Distribution of Green Spaces

Figure 2 (page 19) shows the ward-wise percentage distribution of UGS within the KMC area in six classes. For ease of making the structure, they are combined to form three zonal categories, for which the paper's strategies are framed. They are Category 1: Minimal UGS (0 to 10 percent), Category 2: Moderate UGS (10 to 30 percent), and Category 3: High UGS (above 30 percent). Fifteen of the wards have no open green space, which is alarming, and they also show the unplanned growth of the city. This categorization, by default, gives an idea of the landscape intervention range from quantity (creation of new green areas) to quality (conserving the already existing ones). While Category 1 mostly consists of individual buildings or housings, Category 2 is more related to the neighborhood and community level (local parks, playgrounds, and local water bodies), and Category 3 mostly deals with regional or vast areas of existing green spaces like urban parks or wetlands, which need to be preserved and enhanced in quality.

3.3 Identification of the Barriers

The land use pattern in a city is an outcome of several natural and socio-economic factors, policies and practices, legal and regulatory frameworks, governance systems, financial tools, and informal practices.[22] With the rapid growth of the urban

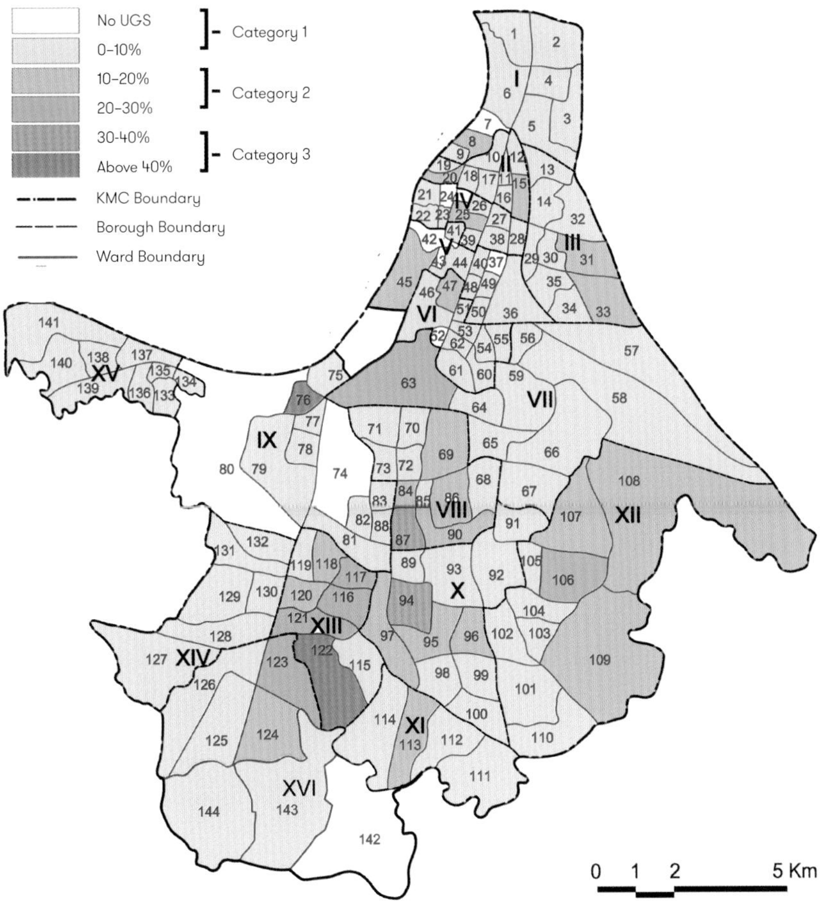

Figure 2
Map of Kolkata showing ward-wise percentage distribution of urban green spaces in 2020

population, the demand for land resources increases. This creates immense pressure on all urban land uses. While there are solutions to counter the problems, there are also some intimidating barriers in the sustainability pathways against the adoption of innovative methods. In India, despite the presence of statutory government bodies like the Ministry of Environment, pollution control boards, and biodiversity boards, there is an absence of efficient policies, governance, and institutional tools at the national, state, and city levels for addressing sustainable land use, urban biodiversity, and climate change issues. The absence of appropriate policies and regulatory frameworks, inefficient administration, and lack of funds and infrastructure are some of them. The paucity of reliable and complete data on the urban sector is another significant barrier to identifying potential interventions; so too is the lack of public participation in the conceptualization and development of projects and proposals. The absence of public interest and the indifference toward public properties discourage the community from accepting and appreciating the government's initiatives.

3.4 Principles of Urban Greening Strategy

3.4.1 Landscape Ecological Approach

The authors suggest a landscape ecological approach toward urban planning, the integration of biodiversity strategies, and the possibility of connectivity. For example, connecting corridors between the existing green areas must be established within the whole urban context. Urban planning guidelines need to be redesigned to emphasize the potentialities and limitations of the natural resources available and establish a connection between the urban dweller and nature. A vernacular and climate-responsive design incorporating socio-cultural-ecological processes, and which also assimilates traditional knowledge is advocated.

3.4.2 Public Participation and Social Inclusion

The suggested strategy recommendations identify stakeholder involvement and public participation as crucial components of integrating green spaces and committing to addressing the needs of all sections of the community. Citizens should be aware of the status and importance of the environment, ecosystem services, and biodiversity. They may be involved in creating and maintaining a status report of local biodiversity and participating in formulating strategies and green city missions. This will, in turn, raise awareness and generate compassion toward nature and biodiversity.

3.4.3 Cost-effective and Efficient Maintenance

The proportion of budget allocated for biodiversity and the environment is usually minimal compared to other categories like road development or street lighting. So, appropriate selections of plant species and easily maintainable landscape designs that can serve multiple ecological functions are preferred. Establishing multiple green spaces throughout the city should be the aim, rather than focusing on just one or a few green spaces. Levying impact fees for community parks or renting them out for cultural functions can also help in their maintenance.

Category	Principle	Area of application
Category 1: wards with "zero" to minimal green space (0 to 10 percent)	Integration of green infrastructure into gray infrastructure	Existing buildings
		Developing buildings
		Joint use of institutional amenities—shared spaces
		Streetscaping
Category 2: wards with moderate amounts of green space (10 to 30 percent)	Integration of green-gray infrastructure	Interstitial vacant spaces
		Neighborhood parks, playgrounds, gardens, and cemeteries
		Local waterbodies
		Gardens around historical or important buildings
Category 3: wards with a high amount of available green space (above 30 percent)	Preservation of already existing green infrastructure	East Kolkata Wetlands, urban parks, and lakefronts
		Riverfronts and canal banks

Table 1
Recommended urban greening strategies for the city of Kolkata

4. Prescribed Urban Greening Strategies

4.1 Category 1: Wards with "Zero" to Minimal Green Space (0 to 10 Percent)—Integration of Green Infrastructure into Gray Infrastructure

The fundamental constraint toward greening these dense wards is the dearth of suitable or potential planting sites. Plantable spaces are often small, isolated, unevenly distributed, and are precious due to scarcity. Even if difficult, it is essential to continually look for opportunities in developing or redeveloping sites and existing buildings, built structures—such as streets, bridges for new planting sites, and the potential for green area networking.

4.1.1 Existing Buildings, Private Properties, Commercial, or Industrial Spaces

When space is scarce and inadequate to provide greenery on the ground level, other greening strategies such as green roofs and façades can be alternative solutions, even if they cannot necessarily be accessed by the public. They can provide various ecosystem services at the site level, like microclimate control, food production, and habitats for urban biodiversity. Green interior spaces in public and commercial buildings can contribute to noise prevention and absorb pollutants and improve indoor air quality. This concept is gaining popularity as it promotes the coexistence of architecture and nature in urban areas, thereby improving the visual and living quality of the city's occupants, and contribute to the city's greenery. Barriers to green roof installations are mainly due to their establishment and maintenance costs, lack of technical information, and concerns about leakage and damage to the roof slab. It is necessary to create some awareness on them and provide public education to advocate their multiple environmental, economic, and social benefits to promote their adoption. This can be through providing technical and price information on various commercial products and methods.

4.1.2 Developing Buildings—Application of Mandatory Green Space Standards

Laying down strict policies for mandatory open spaces in developing buildings may be one strategy to ensure sufficient green space in overcrowded wards. Although these standards do not ensure the quality of these green spaces and make them publicly accessible, they will improve the overall green space provision per inhabitant, thus masking scarcity on the local scale. A variety of small trees or shrub species planted along the boundary walls can also improve the greenery of dense neighborhoods, while using very little space and ensuring low maintenance costs. Incentives could be offered to developers in terms of tax reduction or additional floor area benefits to encourage the implementation of any means of greenery to their structures, such as green walls (both façade-based and ground-based), and green roofs.

4.1.3 Joint Use of Institutional Amenities—Shared Spaces

In some of the wards, there are schools or universities with gardens or playgrounds which can be shared with the people after regular academic hours. These enclosed green areas will provide a breathing space for the residents in congested wards and ensure regular maintenance due to their constant use. It also promotes an awareness of nature, encourages social bonding, and connects people to nature.

4.1.4 Roadside Plantation, Medians, and Roundabouts

Roadside trees are the most cost-effective and obvious way to upgrade the cityscape and provide vital ecosystem services. They occupy little space, share the aboveground space with vehicles and pedestrians, and impart notable scenic and environmental benefits. Even a narrow planting strip of a meter's width can allow the growth of shrubs and small trees. Expanding on this, roadside parking spaces could also accommodate a tree pit that is installed within a metal tree grating. This helps the older parts of Kolkata that, generally, grew organically, where the pavements can sometimes be too narrow, or even occupied by hawkers, resulting in little to no space left to accommodate tree planting. There is also the issue of building awnings, unauthorized projections, and overhead cables above narrow pavements blocking the vertical growth of shrubs and small trees.

4.2 Category 2: Wards with Moderate Amounts of Green Space (10 to 30 Percent)—Integration of Green-gray Infrastructure

4.2.1 Vacant Lots and Parking Areas

Even in the most densely developed wards, there are still several vacant lots, parking areas, rail tracks, utility easements, and corridors between buildings and canal sides that are often overgrown with spontaneous vegetation. These are not coherently managed and hence occupy an uncertain, interstitial niche in the urban matrix. These spaces have much potential to feature greenery if planting is carried out in an organized manner.

4.2.2 Neighborhood Parks, Playgrounds, Gardens, and Cemeteries

Most of the wards in this category have children's parks of variable sizes, which are not maintained properly. Proper maintenance of these parks and converting them into multifunctional areas that cater to all sections of the community will be beneficial to the locals. Because of Kolkata's colonial history, the city is home to several cemeteries that are no longer used for burial. These spaces have a high level of biodiversity and cultural significance, so they are suitable to be integrated into the planning and development of open green spaces. Preserving cemeteries as part of urban green spaces and making them accessible to people can add to the city's visual and recreational greenery and also strengthen heritage.

4.2.3 Local Water Bodies

Ponds and local water bodies (which exist naturally or are artificially created) are an integral part of the people who use them for various purposes like washing, bathing, or to collect water from for other household purposes. However, recently, with the rising demand for real estate, most of them are being filled up or encroached. Maintaining these water bodies to keep benefitting from the various ecosystem services they provide, as well as making them accessible to the local people can benefit the citizens' physical and mental health in the long run.

4.2.4 Gardens Around Historical or Important Buildings

Most heritage buildings are accompanied by gardens which are often neglected or inaccessible to the public. These areas have a high social and cultural significance and are also important for local recreation, tourism, biodiversity, and the urban climate. An initiative from the municipal corporation to revive these gardens and make them accessible to the community can foster a sense of belonging, raise awareness of the city's rich architectural heritage, and at the same time ensure their regular maintenance.

4.3 Category 3: Wards with a High Amount of Available Green Space (Above 30 Percent)—Preservation of Already Existing Green Infrastructure

Preserving the existing natural assets and protecting the eco-sensitive zones in the wards of this category should be the city's foremost duty, in order to protect the vulnerable city from the effects of climate change. These are the wards that consist of ecologically rich natural areas like wetlands, urban parks, riverfronts, and canal banks, which provide biodiverse habitats and essential ecosystem services to the city. The pre-urbanization ecosystem of swamps and native trees should be retained or imitated. Establishing a connection between city dwellers and their natural environment is a prime requirement to address the current environmental crisis that Kolkata faces. This connection needs to be built by understanding natural processes, the inter-relationship of natural environmental components, and the influence of human activity on nature. Urban planning guidelines need to be reworked into ecological planning guidelines that integrate ecological landscape approaches into traditional planning approaches. Integrating culture and nature, promoting interdisciplinary knowledge transfer, and allowing city residents to adapt and live within boundaries set by the natural environment is a way forward to better public health and well-being. A holistic conservation plan for these valuable resources could both improve the ecological function of these sites and make them aesthetically more appealing. Longitudinal features like rivers, canal systems, and major arterial roads and railroads can provide an excellent opportunity to create "ecological corridors" that may connect many urban parks or national lakes into a continuous green belt. Wherever there is no option of a continuous greenbelt, a connection through a roadside plantation may be proposed, which can be easily achieved, even if space is not available.

5. Conclusion

Kolkata's legacy has always been its rich natural heritage consisting of several ecologically rich resources. Unfortunately, the growth of the city was not always on a sustainable trajectory due to various factors. Qualitative and quantitative promotions of its natural features are of utmost importance because of the valuable ecosystem services they impart. Urban greening strategies and interventions need to address the overall context of the urban ecosystem, and integrate with the relevant policies, frameworks, and plans, such as urban masterplans, health and transportation policies, and sustainability and biodiversity strategies. Architects, planners, environmentalists, and administrative bodies need to work in unison for the conservation of green infrastructure and biodiversity. City councilors, together with green groups and concerned citizens, should monitor the development of these sites, so that existing green spaces are preserved as much as possible. To this end, local municipalities could also be rewarded for the maintenance and management of local green spaces.

Developers, too, should provide alternatives or substitutes for the loss of natural greenery, especially where mature trees with a sizeable biomass are concerned, as this impacts substantial aesthetic and environmental benefits. Efficient statutory measures and professional tree-care guidelines should also be adopted to minimize damage to mature trees on the site due to mishandling during the build. The selection of healthy, vibrant, and resistant plants compatible with the location is essential for the area's sustenance, maintenance, local biodiversity, and aesthetic value.

Along with creating new plantable spaces, linear greenway sites—such as riverfronts and canal banks—should be readily utilized for planting opportunities. Existing parks, historical gardens, avenues, promenades, urban squares, cemeteries, botanical and zoological gardens, and special old estates with established vegetation are quantitatively and qualitatively significant urban greenery and make a considerable contribution to the quality of life in towns and cities. More streets in city centers and locations where vehicular traffic is light—which have alternative traffic routes—could be pedestrianized to reduce air and noise pollution and promote green recreational spaces. Another essential condition for the widespread use of public green and open spaces is a good sense of safety, good maintenance, and the cleanliness of these green spaces. Together with a little awareness and efficient management, the points discussed above can positively impact the city's urban future, as well as the health and well-being of the citizens, and set a "green benchmark" for other cities.

Notes

1. Richard Mitchell and Frank Popham, "Effect of Exposure to Natural Environment on Health Inequalities: An Observational Population Study," *The Lancet* 372, no. 9,650 (2008): 1,655–1,660, doi: 10.1016/S0140-6736(08)61689-X.
2. Shah Md. Atiqul Haq, "Urban Green Spaces and an Integrative Approach to Sustainable Environment," *Journal of Environmental Protection* 02, no. 05 (2011): 601–608, doi: https://10.4236/jep.2011.25069.
3. Jasper Schipperijn et al., "Associations Between Physical Activity and Characteristics of Urban Green Space," *Urban for Urban Green* 12 (2013): 109–116.
4. Federal Ministry for the Environment, Nature Conservation, Building and Nuclear Safety, White Paper: *Green Spaces in the City — For a More Liveable Future*, 2018, www.bmub.bund.de/en/service/publications.
5. Marie J. du Toit et al., "Urban Green Infrastructure and Ecosystem Services in Sub-Saharan Africa," *Landscape and Urban Planning* 180 (2018): 249–261, doi: https://doi.org/10.1016/j.landurbplan.2018.06.001.
6. C. Y. Jim, "Sustainable Urban Greening Strategies for Compact Cities in Developing and Developed Economies," *Urban Ecosystem* 16 (2013): 741–761, doi: https://doi.org/10.1007/s11252-012-0268-x.
7. World Health Organization (WHO), "Urban Green Space Interventions and Health: A Review of Impacts and Effectiveness," WHO Regional Office for Europe, Copenhagen, Denmark, 2017.
8. World Health Organization (WHO), "Health Indicators of Sustainable Cities in the Context of the Rio+20 UN Conference on Sustainable Development," Geneva, Switzerland, 2012.
9. Indian Council for Research on International Economic Relations, "Better Cities, Better Growth: India's Urban Opportunity: Synthesis Paper for Policy Makers," New Climate Economy conference, Overseas Resources Institute and Indian Council for Research on International Economic Relations, London, Washington D.C., and New Delhi, 2016, http://newclimateeconomy.report/workingpapers.
10. "Basic Statistics of Kolkata," Kolkata Municipal Corporation official website, https://www.kmcgov.in/KMCPortal/jsp/KolkataStatistics.jsp.
11. TV Ramachandra, Bharath H. Aithal, and M. V. Sowmyashree, "Urban Structure in Kolkata: Metrics and Modeling Through Geo-informatics," *Società Italiana di Fotogrammetria e Topografia (SIFET)* 6 (2014): 229–244, doi: https://10.1007/s12518-014-0135-y.
12. Subham Mukherjee, Wiebke Bebermeier, and Brigitta Schütt, "An overview of the Impacts of Land Use Land Cover Changes (1980–2014) on Urban Water Security of Kolkata," *Land* 7, no. 3 (2018): 1–25, doi: https://10.3390/land7030091.
13. "Study Bares Loss of Open Space in City," *The Telegraph*, February 17, 2017, https://www.telegraphindia.com/states/west-bengal/study-bares-loss-of-open-space-in-city/cid/1397757.
14. Chinmoy Chakraborty, *A Source Book on Environment of Kolkata: Kolkata Environment Improvement Project* (Kolkata, India: Kolkata Municipal Corporation, 2013).
15. Department for International Development, "Climate-friendly Interventions, Policies, Capacity Building and Sustainable Governance (PO7014) (Final Version)," Climate Smart Land Use Planning and Development, Kolkata, 2015.
16. Dhanapal Govindarajulu, "Urban Green Space Planning for Climate Adaptation in Indian Cities," *Urban Climate* 10 (2014): 35-41, doi: http://dx.doi.org/10.1016/j.uclim.2014.09.006.
17. Deepa Padmanaban, "How Indian Cities are Being Shorn of Trees," *India Spend*, March 29, 2016, https://www.indiaspend.com/how-indian-cities-are-being-shorn-of-trees-67909.
18. Prithvijit Mitra, "Open Space Shrinking, City Gasps for Breath," *The Times of India*, May 22, 2013, https://timesofindia.indiatimes.com/city/kolkata/open-space-shrinking-city-gasps-for-breath/articleshow/20188789.cms.
19. "Kolkata City Park – An Initiative", Centre for Contemporary Communication, 2012, http://bhuvan-staging.nrsc.gov.in/projects/parks/rc_bhuvan.php#.
20. Basudeb Bhatta, "Analysis of Urban Growth Pattern Using Remote Sensing and GIS: A Case Study of Kolkata, India," *International Journal of Remote Sensing* 30, no. 118 (2018): 4,733–4,746, doi: 10.1080/01431160802651967.
21. "Urban and Regional Development Plans Formulation and Implementation Guidelines 2015," Government of India, Ministry of Urban Development, Town and Country Planning Organization, https://smartnet.niua.org/sites/default/files/resources/URDPFI%20Guidelines%20Vol%20I.pdf.
22. OECD, "The Governance of Land Use in OECD Countries: Policy Analysis and Recommendations," OECD Publishing, Paris, 2017, http://dx.doi.org/10.1787/9789264268609-en.

Figure Credits

Figure 1: Map of Kolkata showing the spatial distribution of urban green spaces and wetlands in 2020 (authors' drawing).

Figure 2: Map of Kolkata showing ward-wise percentage distribution of urban green spaces in 2020 (authors' drawing).

Analysis of Waterfront Public Space Activities Based on Walking and Space Demand Simulation Using the Public Space in the North Bund of the Huangpu River

GU Zhuoxing, Tongji University, China
ZHANG Ye, National University of Singapore, Singapore
YANG Chunxia*, Tongji University, China
ZHU Wei, Tongji University, China

Abstract

This study uses a multi-agent behavioral simulation method to measure the use of public space on the North Bund waterfront. The multi-agent behavior model is mainly composed of a "scenario model" and a "micro-space selection model," which are used to simulate the user's behavior on how they use the space. The first step was to construct a multi-agent system behavior selection model (scenario behavior model and micro-space selection model) based on three data types consolidated from the North Bund public space: individual behavior, spatial behavior records, and spatial elements. Next, the behavior selection model and the spatial environment were combined to generate a simulation study. The third step derived information data, such as activity density and activity time distribution through spatial grid sampling. The simulation results indicate that the public space of the North Bund has an uneven distribution of activities, uneven distribution of activity time, and an uneven distribution of space utilization.

Keywords

Multi-agent model, scenario model, micro-behavior, activity distribution, design optimization.

Author Information
GU Zhuoxing: guzhuoxing@126.com
ZHANG Ye: akizy@nus.edu.sg
YANG Chunxia (*corresponding author): Yang_achi@163.com
ZHU Wei: weizhu@tongji.edu.cn

Dimension	Focus issue	Imitation object	Simulated environment	Visualize data
City planning	· Urban space expansion, urban form evolution · Land use, land function, land policy evolution · Population migration, evolution of population, living preferences	Citizens, residents, investors	Functional block Urban structure network Urban transportation network	· Urban expansion and morphological evolution · Land use and planning · Population distribution
City design	· Urban regional morphology evolution · Emergency evacuation in urban areas · Urban area business · Recreation and recreational behavior in urban areas	Pedestrian flow Public event crowd Specific activity group	Urban form City function layout	· Spatial evolution pattern · Statistical pattern of business activity distribution · Statistical pattern of leisure activity distribution
Architectural design	· Self-organization of architectural space and form · Evacuation of interior space · Evaluation of space function and form utility	Evacuate people Specific activity group	Space plane form Function layout Supporting facilities Space logo	· Evolution of spatial structure · Function evolution · Activity distribution pattern
Public space	· Public space recreation and leisure behavior · Public space evacuation and safety	Evacuate people Specific activity group	Spatial structure Function layout Space logo Facilities	· Classification and distribution pattern of leisure activities · Evacuation route

Table 1
Application of multi-agent
behavior simulation

1. Introduction

New urban science and its related theories have changed the observation and research perspectives of urban spaces. Over the years, more research has shifted from traditional classifications and qualitative analysis to focusing on the inherent intricate network structure and the interaction mechanism between these network structures.[1] Establishing the mapping relationship of different information networks in mathematical models or computer models has become a common subject of system simulation research. A public space and its users can be seen as two independent system networks, and these networks can be gradually "decomposed." There are axis systems, square systems, functional configuration systems, and so on, in the public space, and the users themselves can also be "decomposed" into categories of different of needs.[2] These systems interact and interweave in the real world, resulting in a public space activity scene.[3]

The research in this paper used the "decomposition" of the spatial design element system and the behavioral activity system to enable the multi-agent system, to establish a self-organized coupling model, and to visually realize the spatial measurement results. In the construction of dynamic models, the uncertainty and diversity of user behavior in mesoscale or micro-space pose challenges for multi-agent behavior simulation. Taking waterfront public spaces as an example—specifically, the North Bund public space—for the purpose of this study, the user activity type scenarios and site preferences were summarized into the activity demand set and the micro-space selection set; this has become the practice to explore and simulate the behavior of users in such waterfront public spaces. Through these methods, the multi-agent behavior simulation of the waterfront public space provides a refined measurement basis for the post-use evaluation of the space.

2. A Brief Overview of Waterfront Space Micro-behavior and Multi-agent Space Behavior Simulation

2.1 Research and Development of a Waterfront Public Space and its Activities

A waterfront public space is a special category of urban public space, and is seen in many cities that rely on rivers, lakes, and oceans to develop these spaces, often becoming the core of local areas in the city. These spaces have usually also undergone "de-industrialization," transforming from industry-oriented and function-oriented spaces to complex urban development spaces.[4] Waterfront public spaces in major cities in the world have become important open places in citizens' lives and have become important "urban living rooms."[5] Therefore, more and more studies have been exploring the inter-relationships of user spaces in waterfront public spaces on macro and micro scales.

2.1.1 Research on the Scale of Macro-planning

In the urban regional space, the connectivity and accessibility of a waterfront public space and urban hinterland are often hot topics of discussion. Priscilla Ananian, in her journal article (2022), took Montreal's waterfront as an example, focusing on the traffic behavior in the pedestrian traffic space between the edge of the waterfront and the hinterland of the waterfront.[6] Quentin Stevens, in his article (2006), used the core squares and landmark squares in the inner city riverside cultural and recreational areas (both referred to as "Southbank") in Australia's two major cities—Melbourne and Brisbane—by observing the extensive leisure activities and their complex organization and interaction behaviors.[7]

2.1.2 Research on Refined Spatial Scale

The types of activities and people in waterfront public spaces are complex and diverse, and with time fluctuations, the elements in these spaces have also become rich and diverse. Therefore, refined observation and recording methods are needed to perform an effective analysis.[8]

The renovation of the urban brownfield waterfront in Tallinn, Estonia was carried out in 2011. During this period, the spatial form of the waterfront beach, waterfront walks, large rocks on the beach, seating seats, convenient changing spaces, and other spatial facilities were used to refine the space.[9] A 2005 survey of urban waterfront public activity spaces in Tianjin, China, sampled the actual situation of waterfront space activities from the perspectives of activity forms, children's activity sites, and subspaces, and summarized the importance of open space, the strengthening of ground paving design, noise control, attention to the elderly, and diversity.[10]

The research on Pontianak Waterfront, Indonesia, investigated the relationship between the layout of the hawker plane in a waterfront public space, as well as the relationship between tour and consumption activities on a tourist landscape, and proposed design and management measures, including the concept of regional zoning, circulation settings, visual quality improvement, and relocation.[11]

Crowd activities within a waterfront public space showcase the space's unique leisurely ambiance, the freedom of movement within the area, as well as the landscape of the waterfront space on a complex basis with unique characteristics. Therefore, the refined use assessment of waterfront spaces should be based on the collection and analysis of micro-behavior data, and the elements of space design that need to be improved and optimized to align with the characteristics and needs of a waterfront public space.

2.2 Spatial Analysis Application of Multi-agent Model

The development of computer technology provides more methods and tools to refine the relationship between space and behavior. Among them, behavior simulation has become more common.[12] Through computer simulation, researchers can not only simulate and demonstrate behavioral models (mathematical models, theoretical models, and such) based on space experience, but they can also change model parameters to verify more assumptions and conduct space use assessments. On top of that, this process can be intuitively reflected through more flexible visualization technology. With its own flexibility and openness, the multi-agent system can establish credible mapping to reflect the user and the material space environment, and simulate their interaction.[13]

2.2.1 Spatial Simulation and Measurement of Urban Planning

An important link in the simulation of urban regional morphology is the establishment of a spatial evolution mechanism, which can be based on the summary of the inter-evolution relationship between population, industry, and major events, and their urban network structure, as well as transportation and commerce.

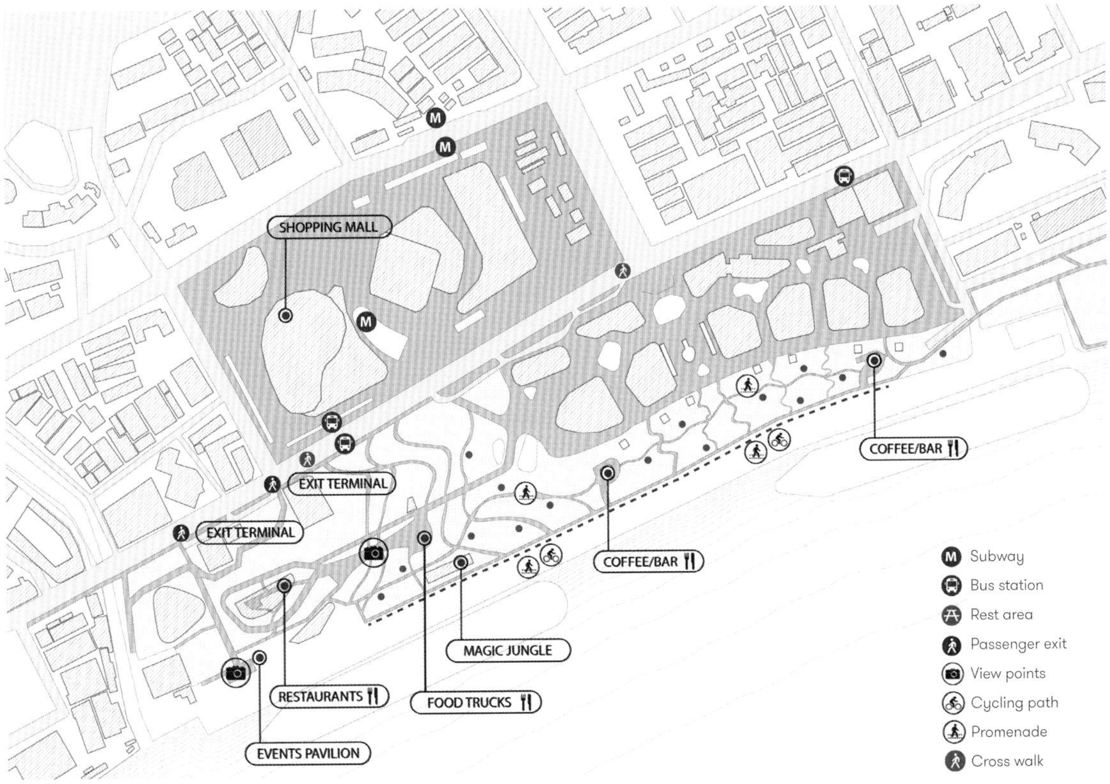

Figure 1
Public spaces in the North Bund, Shanghai

Activity classification	Simulation content	Specific behavior	Social factors	Environmental factors
Waterfront activities	Touch the water	Fishing, wading about in the shallow water	Allow a small number of people around	Available water area
	Observe The Water	Viewing spots, boating		
Landscape activity	Relaxing, people-watching	Taking photos, relaxing, people-watching	Allow a small number of people around	Iconic site
	Snap photos (selfies, group photos)	Snapping photos of landmarks		Iconic scenery
Recreational activities	Leisure, relaxation	Sitting, lying down	Hope no one is close by	Recreational facilities Greening enclosure conditions
Consumer activity	Consumption	Eating, shopping	Unaffected	Consumer facilities
Cultural activities	Watching	Watching street performances, browsing display posters	Allow a small number of people around	Cultural facilities
	Visiting	Visiting exhibition/s	Hope there are people mingling about	
Fitness activity	Fitness facilities	Aerobics, fitness corners	Hope there are more people around	Fitness facilities
	Recreational fitness	Roller skating, rollerblading, jogging	Unaffected	Running track Guide points

Table 2
Classification of public space activities in the North Bund, Shanghai

Building a simulation evolution model in the platform of the agent provides a visual analysis approach for the mutual evolution relationship of urban network systems.[14] Different urban areas, different urban functional areas, and streets of different nature should form independent and distinctive spatial evolution rules. The advantage of the multi-agent system is in being able to apply different rules in the same simulation to form an overall evolution effect.[15]

In the mutual game evolution mechanism of urban land, policies, users, investors, and environment (and many other factors), the multi-agent system is used to establish the relationship between land-related subjects and the environment.[16] The change in urban residential areas reflect the growth of the urban population, and the decision on housing location reflects the key factors of population migration in this process. Researchers usually construct self-selected multi-agents based on these factors to make predictions for urban population growth, as well as determine the limitations of related spatial planning.[17]

2.2.2 Spatial Simulation and Measurement of Urban Areas

With regards to the scale of urban areas, local areas, and characteristic areas, multi-agent systems are mostly used to construct the measurement research of the relationship between user behavior, demand and spatial evacuation, spatial function, and spatial form. In earlier applications, the evacuation of urban areas was the theme.[18]

Compared with the simulation of evacuation behaviors, commercial and recreational behaviors widely exist in the external environment of the city, and a multi-agent system is required to be able to simulate the user's behavior selection process.[19] Consumer behavior is also affected by the surrounding environment. The relevant characteristics of a public space (spatial organization, spatial scale, spatial location, and type of emergencies) can be simplified into a system of model spatial expressions, which can be summarized as channels, conveniences, nodes, and exports.[20]

Compared with consumer behaviors and other more purposeful behaviors, spatial recreational behaviors are more complex. Users often spontaneously carry out many activities in an urban space, such as watching, staying, and walking.[21] Through the free behavior combination mode, the multi-agent system shows a wealth of free behavior modes in the urban open public space, and forms a self-organized activity density, activity type, and location distribution, thereby providing a public space behavior system and a network of spatial elements. The interaction relationship (spatial axis sequence, public square, spatial scale, and spatial form) provides a clear measurement.[22]

2.2.3 Spatial Simulation and Measurement of Architecture

When using the interaction of multi-agents in the micro site for building-scale morphology generation, the functional requirements of architectural design are usually coded into multi-agent game rules. The same types of functions attract and gather each other, and the differences created are large. Functions are mutually exclusive and separated, forming a building space structure and functional organization that evolve on their own, and eventually reach a stable state, and finally form the building material space plan.[23] Similar to urban space, the evacuation efficiency and congestion in architectural space are also the research hotspots in traffic buildings, and the simulation of evacuation in the buildings is closely related to the subtle perception of the building space by

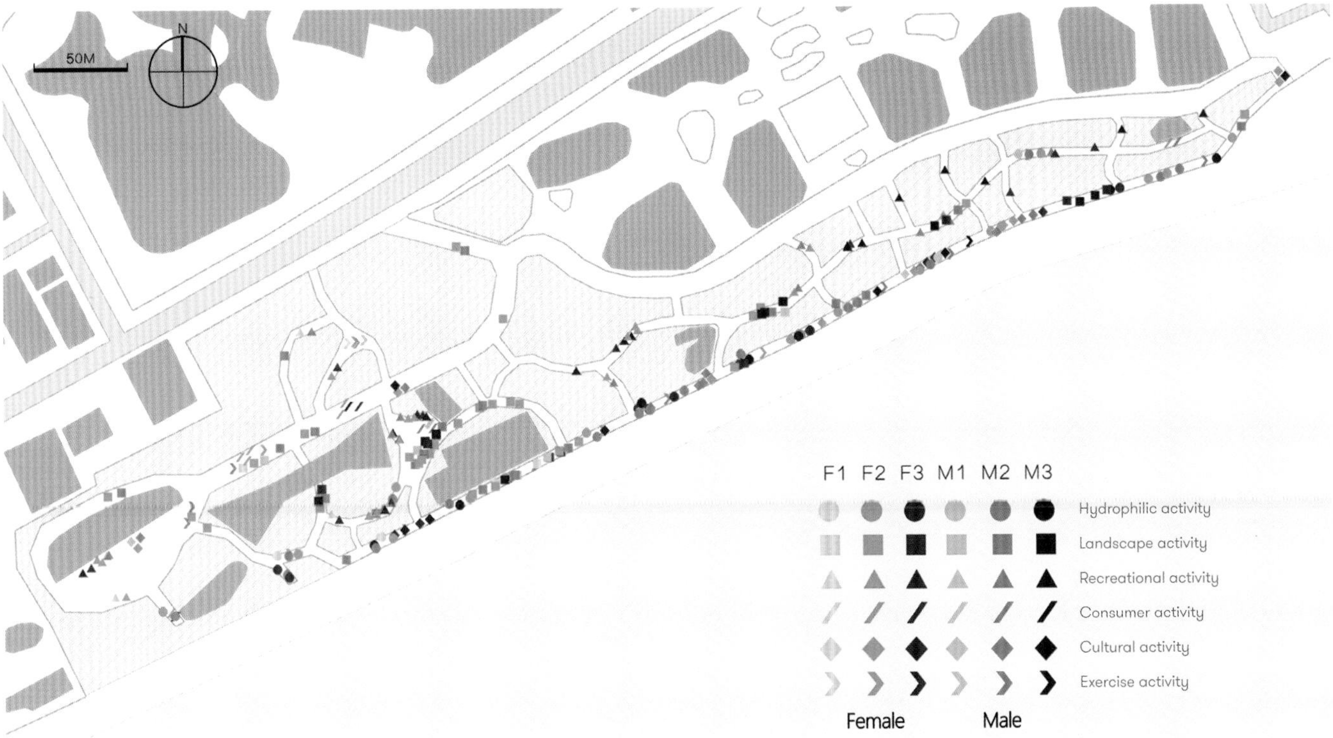

Figure 2
Statistics on the distribution of public space activities in the North Bund, Shanghai

the crowd, the construction of evacuation paths, and the guidance of the interior of the space.[24]

2.2.4 Spatial Simulation and Measurement of Outdoor Public Space

In outdoor public behavior simulation research, the public space behavior and environment are generally solved through the steps of behavior data collection, multi-agent behavior construction, outdoor environment space construction, multi-agent interaction with the environment, distribution pattern, related problem analysis, and so on.[25]

Leisure and recreational activities have a strong randomness, but in outdoor public spaces, such as urban activity squares, waterfront public spaces, and urban pedestrian streets, leisure and recreational activities form the main subjects. Also, the amount of leisure activities is closely related to the overall vitality of the space and the overall economic benefits of the space.[26] The user behavior model can be formed according to the user's own attributes and usage preference data, and the behavior needs of multi-agents can be formed through subjective behavior intentions. Then, multi-agents and public spaces (square space facilities, spatial layout, facility configuration, leisure trails, and such) are simulated and interacted to obtain a detailed spatial behavior distribution.[27] The evacuation simulation of a public space also reflects the refined control characteristics of multi-agents.[28]

It can be seen that the multi-agent model is widely used in urban planning, urban design, architectural design, and public space research. Its main operation mode is to respectively map space users with the physical space environment (material spatial form, spatial function configuration, natural ecological landscape, and such). Finally, researchers observe the evolution patterns and statistical data on spatial form, spatial function, spatial activity, crowd evacuation, and spatial microclimate (Table 1, page 24).

3. Construction of Multi-agent Model of Waterfront Public Space Behavior Activities

This research first summarized the types of activities and spatial elements of users in the space through data collection on the actual site (the Huangpu River, North Bund). Then, a walking particle system with demand behavior was built through multi-agent simulation technology. Finally, in the walking simulation model, the spatial vitality of the experiment site was measured from multiple angles to analyze the advantages and disadvantages of the space design.[29]

3.1 Research Site Data Analysis

In 2018, Shanghai completed the pedestrian space of the waterfront public space along the Huangpu River, which is 45 kilometers long. Numerous public spaces, public space facilities, pedestrian spaces, public activity squares, and cultural space facilities were set up along the way for citizens to "play" in and use.[30] In order to simulate the spatial behavior of this type of waterfront public space, it was necessary to count the distribution and quantity data of the actual space facilities, as well as the space activity data in the actual situation in order to establish a true simulation model.

3.1.1 Site Environment

The North Bund is located in the downtown area of Shanghai on the Huangpu River; the landmark towers in the Lujiazui area and the old shipyard financial city can be observed

	Landscape leisure	Waterfront-oriented	Culture-oriented	Rest-oriented	Sports consumption	Passing through
Activity demand	Average occurrence of activities within block size 200 by 200 meters					
Waterfront activities	1.52	2.56	1.95	1.75	1.27	1.00
Landscape activity	2.10	1.67	0.86	0.12	0.00	1.07
Recreational activities	2.59	1.11	0.86	2.44	0.40	0.27
Consumer activity	0.00	0.81	0.00	0.00	0.87	0.00
Fitness activity	0.14	0.07	0.19	0.00	0.87	0.20
Cultural activities	1.03	1.11	2.48	0.62	0.13	0.20

Table 3
Activity scenarios and activity characteristics

Average number of activities				
	Average value	Standard deviation	Influence trend	Parameter setting value
Waterfront activity point	2.11	1.133	Attract	2–3
Landscape activity spot	1.71	1.384	Attract	2
Recreation point	1.48	1.313	Reject	0–1
Consumption activity point	2.25	2.630	No obvious correlation	No obvious correlation
Cultural event spot	3.55	1.635	Attract	3–4
Fitness activity point	1.54	1.450	Reject	0–1

Table 4
Number of people around micro-activity space

along the coast. The public space of the North Bund contains facilities for commerce and entertainment, and it also features supporting facilities, enabling citizens to enjoy convenient urban services. The surrounding transportation facilities are also complete and convenient; it is close to the subway station, there are many bus lines passing through the area, and corresponding parking facilities are also provided. Overall, it is very convenient for other areas within the city to access this area.[31]

The public space of the North Bund is adjacent to the Huangpu River and its interior is mainly composed of walking roads, various recreational facilities, entertainment and landscape facilities, cultural facilities, and catering and F&B facilities (Figure 1, page 25). In the construction of a multi-agent simulation system, it was necessary to shape the simulated space environment according to the real situation of the site in order to form an evaluation of the existing real space design, as well as the functional planning.

3.1.2 Field Activity Data

Multi-agent individuals mainly simulate users' spatial behavior in the simulation, so it was necessary to collect users' behavior characteristics in the sample space to construct the correct multi-agent behavior. In this study, in view of the common behavioral characteristics in waterfront public spaces, and according to the social and spatial properties of public activities, the existing public space activities of the North Bund were mainly divided into six types: water activities, landscape activities, recreational activities, consumer activities, sports activities, and cultural activities (Table 2, page 26).

For purposes of gathering data statistics, the time period of 4:00 pm to 5:00 pm on weekends was selected for actual activity marking statistics in the public space (Figure 2, page 27), and three weekend crowd activity statistics from mid-April 2021 were selected and superimposed to form a comprehensive waterfront space activity sample.[32] The statistics show that different space facilities, such as seats, viewing points that overlook the water, landscape facilities, and so on have different appeals to different users. Congestion in the space or interference with users' mutual behavior was also noted, indicating that the local public space has the potential to be transformed and improved further.

3.2 Multi-agent Model Construction

Based on the field space and behavior data of the North Bund, a unique multi-agent behavior simulation was needed to respond to the behavior of existing public space users. To this end, the researchers conducted 124 follow-up studies on users who entered the public space in the North Bund, and recorded the frequency and duration of each user's waterfront activities, landscape activities, recreational activities, consumption activities, fitness activities, and cultural activities.

Finally, through cluster analysis and correlation analysis, a spatial scenario behavior model and a micro-behavior model were formed, which enables the agent to map the behavior of visitors in the public space of the North Bund.[33, 34]

3.2.1 Scenario Behavior Model

During the tracking behavior recording process, each observed person moved freely in the waterfront public space of the North Bund without knowing it. Investigators recorded the number and frequency of various activities carried out by users. According to the clustering algorithm, the behaviors and activities in the public space in the North Bund were divided into six categories—waterfront, landscape, recreation, consumption, fitness, and culture—with each category featuring different characteristics. Users who sought landscape-based leisure have the highest demand for leisure activities and landscape activities. Waterfront-oriented people have the highest frequency of waterfront activities carried out in the site, which are at times also accompanied by certain landscape activities. Cultural groups mainly engage in cultural activities; those are also accompanied by certain water activities. Recreation-type people mainly rely on leisure activities. Sports-oriented people have the highest demand for fitness activities, and also have strong waterfront needs. The passing-through crowd has a low demand for activities in all aspects, but has certain needs for waterfront and landscape interaction (Table 3, page 28).

It can be seen that the six scenarios' behavior models summarize, to a certain extent, the personal preferences and needs of users in the North Bund waterfront public space, and explain the probability of different types of people carrying out different activities within the site.

3.2.2 Agent Micro-behavior Model

The activities of users in public spaces are not only affected by space demands, but also by the actual social and spatial elements in the site.[35] Therefore, the researchers summed up the average number of people active near various living spaces in the North Bund, as well as their influence on the activities, and established a model for the selection of micro-activity spaces (Table 4, page 28).

According to the social distance theory of crowd activities, 5 to 10 meters was selected as the statistical range of people around the activity space.[36] In the interaction with the waterfront activity space, the users tended to choose spaces that allowed maximum visibility of the water surface, where they could look out at the iconic landscape, and which had only two to three other users. When it came to the choice of landscape activity space, users always tended to select activity spaces with less than two people. Where the rest of the behavior is concerned, people seemed more unaccepting of other users in the area and preferred to choose activity spaces with the least number of people around. However, the number of people around the consumption space was less relevant in the demand for consumption activities, so the best option overall would be to set areas within according to the principle of avoiding crowds. When the number of people is around three to four users, the cultural activity space has the strongest attraction. People also preferred to choose a space with fewer people around for fitness activities. Therefore, in Figure 3, in the choice of a waterfront activity space, A, B, and C are all within the perception range of the agent, but A and C are abandoned because they do not meet the optimal judgment of the waterfront activity model. The agent finally chooses B for waterfront activities.

4. Behavior Simulation and Spatial Analysis of the Waterfront Public Space of the North Bund

Based on the analysis that is based on the actual spatial activity data and behavior tracking data of the North Bund site, the study was able to construct a multi-intelligence scenario behavior

Figure 3
Micro-activity and spatial selection model

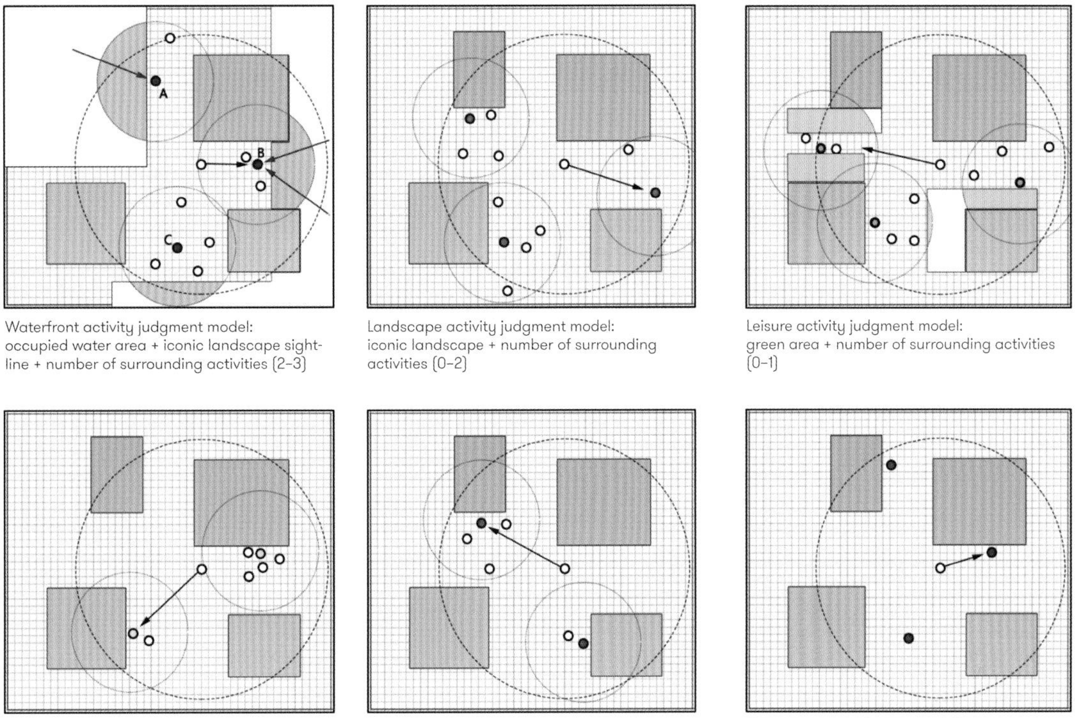

Waterfront activity judgment model: occupied water area + iconic landscape sight-line + number of surrounding activities (2–3)

Landscape activity judgment model: iconic landscape + number of surrounding activities (0–2)

Leisure activity judgment model: green area + number of surrounding activities (0–1)

Consumption activity judgment model: consumption facilities + number of services (0–2)

Cultural activity judgment model: cultural facilities + number of visitors (3–4)

Sports activity judgment model: sports facilities + number of visitors (0–1)

The judgment radius of the fixed activity point is a small-scale interaction distance of 5 to 10 meters model and a micro-behavior model. In order to simulate the crowd and realize the interactive simulation of the site and the activity, the spatial grid sampling method can be used to record the corresponding activity data characterization to support the spatial analysis.[37]

4.1 Simulation and Data Logging

4.1.1 Simulated Environment

The public space of the North Bund extends linearly along the middle section of the Huangpu River, and its block shape can be roughly accommodated within a rectangular area of 200 by 800 meters. For the convenience of research and statistical analysis, the plot is divided into four rectangular site ranges of 200 by 200 meters (Figure 4). Buildings, activity space barriers, and waterfront, landscape, consumption, fitness, and cultural spaces are arranged in each plot according to the actual layout. Within those, the building space and activity space barriers define the space that users can use for walking. The activity attraction points (activity points) are arranged according to the actual concentration of waterfront, landscape, consumption, fitness, and cultural activities in the site survey and the actual site facilities.

4.1.2 Data Sampling Grid

According to the scale of the site model, grid systems of 200 by 200 meters, 50 by 50 meters, and 10 by 10 meters were used to record the activity data of the agent (Figure 5). Among them, the 50-meter grid reflects the relationship between spatial design changes and activity changes in the microscopic area, and the 10-meter grid delicately reflects the relationship between activities and site details on the social scale of the crowd.[38, 39]

4.1.3 Multi-agent Behavior Flow

In the program, a behavioral flow is established for the multi-agent system based on the behavioral probability generated by the scenario model. Each agent particle in the process starts from the beginning and decides to execute a scenario or continue to move according to the scenario model. In the process, only fitness activities do not require micro-behavior choices and directly participate in activities. For other types of activities, the agent needs to select the particular activity point based on the micro-behavior model. After completing all the scenario requirements, the agent particles may choose to leave the venue and end the tour process (Figure 6, page 31).

4.1.4 Simulation Iteration and Behavior Trajectory

The initial operation of the model sets crowd density limits in different site areas to simulate the actual number of people. According to the actual survey data of the site, the simulated maximum number of people in sites I, II, III, and IV is set to 30, 50, 20, and 20 people, respectively. According to the simulation iteration process, to observe the changes in the number of activities and the changes in the number of records, the number of activities will be limited after a certain stage of growth. This is because the number of people entering the site and the number of people leaving the site have reached a dynamic balance. This dynamic balance indicates the simulation. The model can correspond to the dynamic balance of the number of people on the real site, and the simulation results have certain statistical and

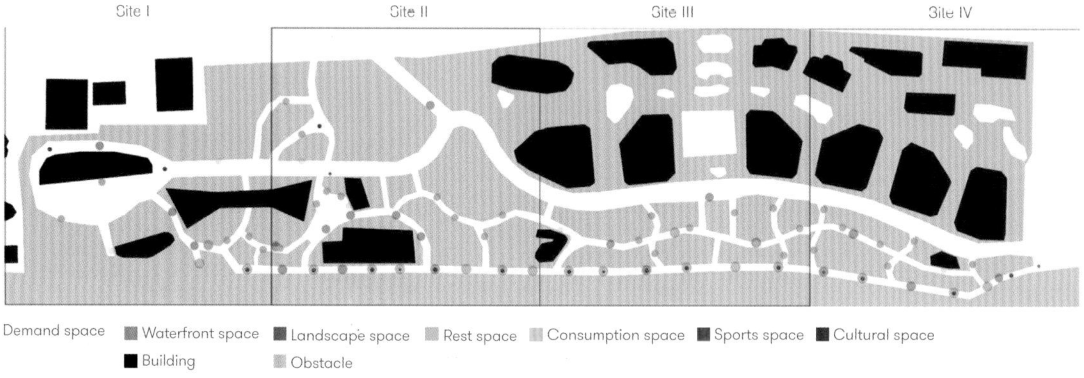

Figure 4
Simulated space environment construction

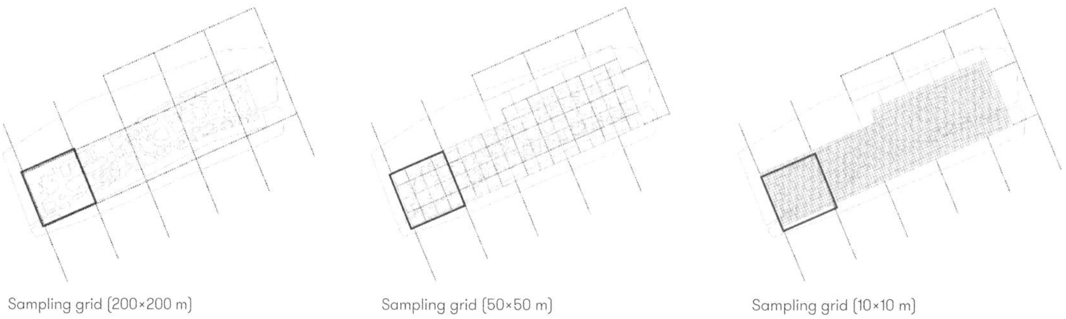

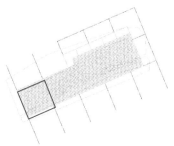

Figure 5
Spatial sampling grid design

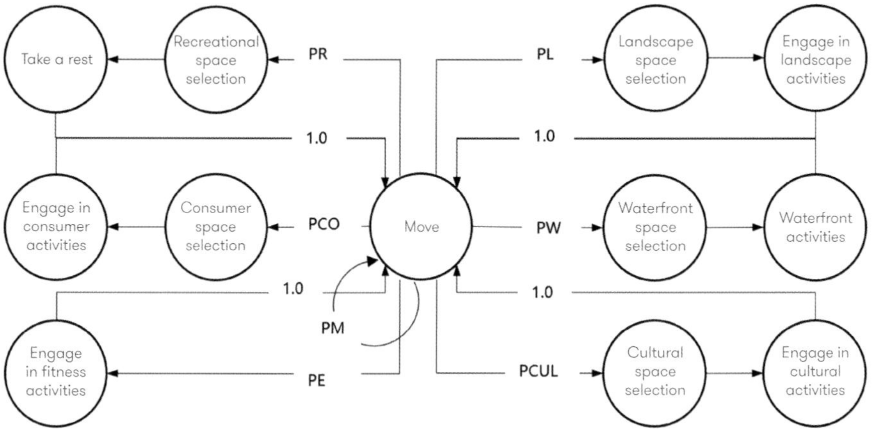

PW, PL, PR, PCO, PE, PCUL, PM denote the probabilities of waterfront demand, landscape demand, leisure demand, consumer demand, sports demand, and moving demand in the scenario model, and the total is 1

Figure 6
Multi-agent behavior flow

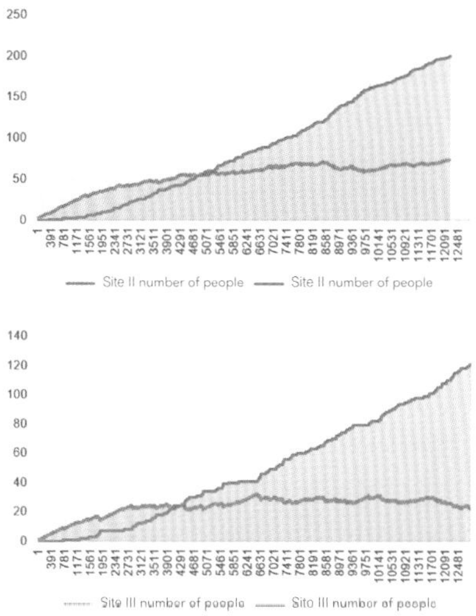

Figure 7
Simulation of headcount monitoring

analytical significance.[40] The number of people recorded is the cumulative number of people who have completed the simulation and walked out of the site. The more people recorded, the larger the data sample size of the activity record (Figure 7).[41]

The multi-agent particles that simulate the actors leave precise behavior trajectories in the space model (Figure 8, page 32). The behavioral trajectory provides a basic analysis pattern for space activities. From the trajectory pattern of this simulation experiment, it can be seen that some loop designs in plot I have not been implemented in behavioral activities, and most people did not choose to take the loop. A common problem in plots I, III, and IV is that, on the whole, the flow of people on the site is concentrated in the linear space where the waterfront space is the most present, and some interesting branch paths in the hinterland have fewer pedestrians.

4.2 Site Activity Distribution Analysis

4.2.1 Activity Point Frequency Statistics

The simulation process recorded the number of activities at each attraction point, which reflected the frequency that each activity point was used (Figure 9, page 32). The waterfront activity points are distributed in the linear space along the river and the waterfront activity points at the head and tail of this linear space are visited more frequently. The activity points in the middle are more evenly visited. This result is caused by the crowded flow of people in the linear activity area and interference from other activities. The same situation also appears in the statistics of the frequency of visits to the cultural activity points and recreational activity points. Because the function of the activity points in the edge is relatively single, the activity points in the edge of the site are visited more frequently. It is more obvious that the curved branches in the hinterland space and the activity points in the linear space are lower and visited more evenly. However, a small number of activity points with multiple functions are visited more frequently.

4.2.2 Overall Distribution of Site Activities

From the statistics of the total number of activities, the number of waterfront activities and recreational activities in the simulated space is the highest, followed by the number of landscape activities (Figure 10, page 32). Consumption activities and fitness activities are less, and there is a certain amount of cultural activities. Adding to that, the number of activities in sites I and II is relatively high, while the number of activities in sites III and IV is relatively low. Comparing with the activity plan, it is found that the uneven distribution of activities in sites I and II is more obvious and the activity areas on some branch roads are seldom used; the number of activities in sites III and IV are evenly distributed. In general, the amount of activity on the periphery of the site is high, but unevenly distributed, and the amount of activity in the hinterland of the site is lower and more evenly distributed.

4.3 Activity Density and Activity Time Analysis

4.3.1 Activity Density Analysis

In the simulation, the number of people was recorded through the 50-by-50-mtere and 10-by-10-meter grid systems, thereby forming a space activity density heat map, reflecting the true distribution of space activities. It can be seen from the 50-by-50-meter grid pattern that the spatial activities in the

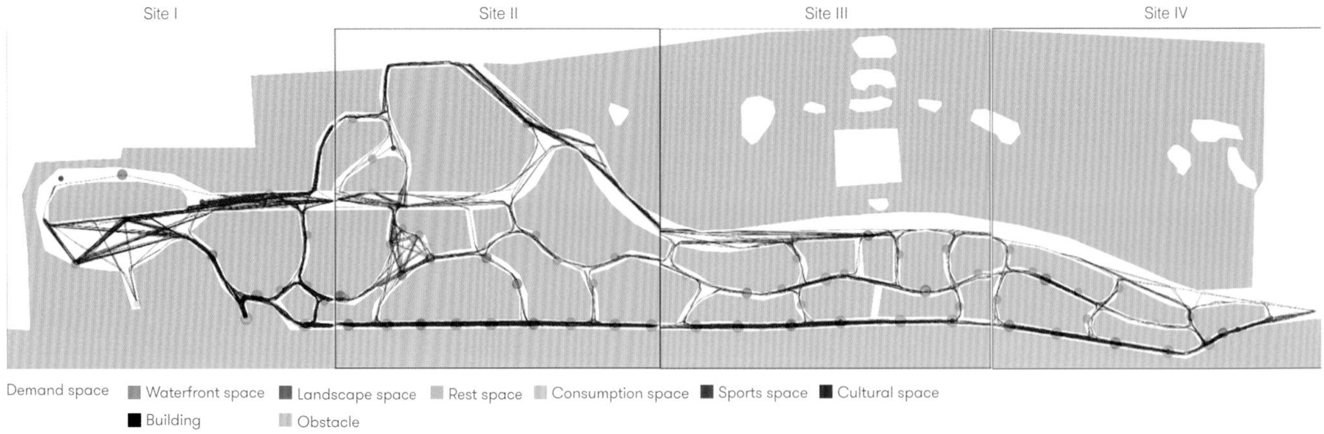

Figure 8
Activity track record

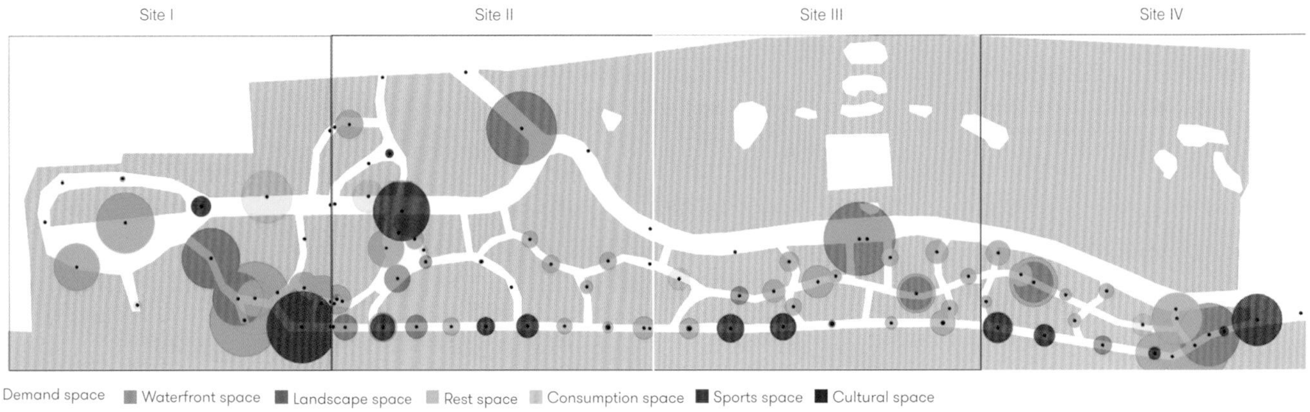

Figure 9
Rate of visits to activity points

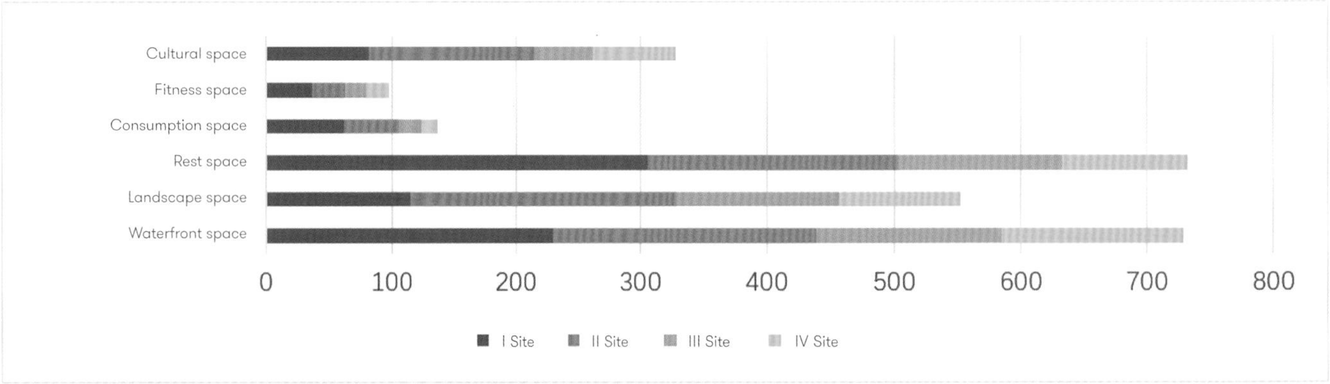

Figure 10
Total activity record

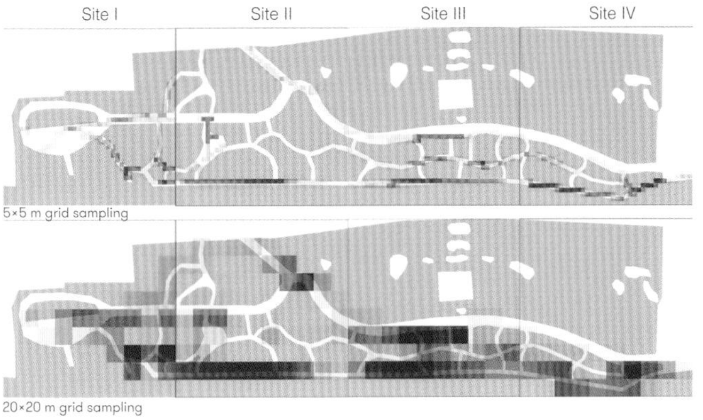

Figure 11
Heat map of activity density distribution

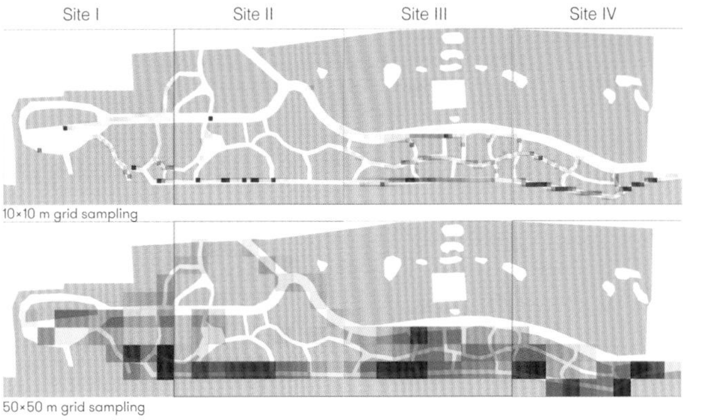

Figure 12
Activity time distribution heat map

North Bund are concentrated in several key areas. Most of these areas are related to the development of waterfront activities, indicating that waterfront activities have a strong attraction for people entering this area. However, some interesting branch roads and fork road areas have low activity density and there is room for space improvement (Figure 10, page 32).

From the 20-by-20-mtere grid pattern, it can be seen that the function setting of the denser activity area is more complex and the spatial scale and form are more concentrated. If a more flexible spatial structure is adopted and the spatial functions are dispersed and the spatial scale is appropriately relaxed, it will be more conducive to easing concentrated spatial activities. Branch roads and fork roads with fewer activities can readjust the spatial shape and space-oriented design, and increase or adjust the function configuration to attract certain activities and make the overall utilization rate of the space more balanced (Figure 11).

4.3.2 Activity Time Analysis

In the simulation, the activity time of the crowd was recorded by the 50-by-50-meter and 10-by-10-meter grid systems, thereby forming a heat map of activity time density, reflecting the difference of activity time in different regions. From the 50-by-50-meter grid heat map, it can be seen that the activity time is roughly the same as the activity density trend. However, it can be seen from the 10-by-10-meter grid heat map that the cumulative activity time intensity of plots III and IV is greater than those of plots I and II. In addition, the activity time distribution of plots I and II is relatively concentrated, while the activity time distribution of plots III and IV is relatively uniform. This is due to the fact that the layout of the activity facilities in plots I and II are scattered and because most of them are independent facilities, such as cultural facilities, fitness facilities, and landscape facilities, while the main activity facilities in plots III and IV are recreational facilities, and the layout is moderately spaced. The design trend of different areas make the distribution of activity time different (Figure 12).

By comparing the activity density distribution map and the activity time distribution map, it can be found that the actual use of the site is affected by the density of the activity plane and the time of the activity. Different types of activities extend for different durations, so different activities should be guided to match each other in space design to form a more reasonable activity time distribution.

5. Conclusion

This study used agent behavior simulation to visualize the space usage in waterfront public spaces. According to the activity data and behavior tracking data of the waterfront public space on the North Bund in Shanghai, user activities in the venue are classified into six categories: waterfront, landscape, recreation, consumption, fitness, and cultural. Based on the activity data, a situational behavior model and a microscopic behavior model were constructed, and the behavioral scenarios were classified into: landscape/leisure-oriented, waterfront-oriented, cultural-oriented, leisure-oriented, sports/consumption-oriented, and passing-through.

In the simulation results, the spatial form and function were analyzed by using the site activity distribution data, activity density data, and activity time distribution data. It is found that in the public space of the North Bund, the central hinterland and the edge of the site have different distribution forms, and the activities at the edge of the site are more concentrated, and the degree of functional complexity is weak. The central hinterland activity distribution is relatively even, and the functional compound degree is high. From the perspective of activity distribution time, activities in the peripheral area are more concentrated, while the central hinterland activity time distribution is more uniform.

According to the distribution of spatial activities shown by the simulation results, the public space in the North Bund can be improved according to the following strategies: first, from the overall spatial planning, attention can be paid to the discrete layout of functional areas, so that the spatial scale and functional settings can penetrate each other. In this way, the mutual independence and concentration of waterfront space and rest space can be avoided, so as to guide the mutual penetration and distribution of activities. Further, attention should be paid to avoid the excessive or centralized arrangement of compound function points in the layout of spatial functions, so that the activities are concentrated and the spatial functions are limited. And an appropriate distance should be set between independent function points to form a network system, so as to ensure the uniform distribution of activity density and activity time. Finally, the shape and connection of some micro spaces should be matched with the overall pedestrian flow system to ensure that branch roads and fork roads are easy to find and use, as well as to improve the overall space utilization rate.

The agent scenario model and micro-behavior model proposed in this study are both simplifications of real behavior data, which reflect the real spatial behavior to a certain extent, but cannot represent the spatial behavior itself. Also, this study is mainly based on the simulation of plane activities and plane space behavior, so the method of this study is more suitable for relatively flat sites. This study has formed an ideal crowd simulation model of the waterfront public space on the North Bund and can record the detailed data of crowd activities within the site, which is convenient for space researchers.

Notes

1. Michael Batty, The New Science of Cities (MIT Press, 2013), 33–34.
2. Robert H. Samet,"Complexity: The science of Cities and Long-range Futures," *Futures 47* (2013): 49–58.
3. Jan Gehl and Lars Gemzøe, *Public Spaces – Public Life* (Kbh: Arkitektens Forlag, 2004), 88–92.
4. Wang Jianguo, Lu Zhipeng, "A Historic Review of World Urban Waterfront Development," *City Planning Review* 25, no. 7 (2001): 41–46.
5. Zhang Tingwei, "Decentralization, Localization, and the Emergence of a Quasi-participatory Decision-making Structure in Urban Development in Shanghai," *International Planning Studies* 7, no. 4 (2002): 303–323.
6. Priscilla Ananian, Valérie Ebacher, and Ariane Perras, "Reconnecting Waterfronts and Central Neighborhoods: The Lessons to be Learned from User Behavior for the Redesign of Public Spaces, " *Journal of Urban Design 27*, no. 1 (2022): 110–129.
7. Quentin Stevens, "The Design of Urban Waterfronts: A Critique of Two Australian 'Southbanks', " *The Town Planning Review*, (2006): 173–203.
8. Gehl and Gemzøe, *Public Spaces – Public Life.*
9. Anna-Liisa Unt and Simon Bell, "The Impact of Small-scale Design Interventions on the Behavior Patterns of the Users of an Urban Wasteland, " *Urban Forestry & Urban Greening 13*, no. 1 (2014): 121–135.
10. Lian Yongzhe, *Research on Environmental Behavior of Waterfront Open Space in Tianjin*, (Tianjin University, 2005), 68–73.
11. Akbar E. P., Y. Ratih, and C. Destria, "The Concept of Street Vendors Arrangement in the Waterfront, " *IOP Conference Series: Earth and Environmental Science*, vol. 780, no. 1, (IOP Publishing, 2021).
12. Nigel Gilbert, Computational Social Science: Agent-based Social Simulation, Agent-based Modelling and Simulation (University of Surrey, 2007), 115–134.
13. Eric Bonabeau, "Agent-based Modeling: Methods and Techniques for Simulating Human Systems, " *Proceedings of the National Academy of Sciences* 99, no. 3 (2002): 7,280–7,287.
14. Liu Jie, *Research on the Dynamic Mechanism of the Spatial Evolution of Open Cities Based on Multi-agent Simulation* (Tianjin University, 2017), 107–111.
15. Julien Perret et al., "A Multi-agent System for the Simulation of Urban Dynamics, " 10th European Conference on Complex Systems, 2010.
16. Stefano Picascia, Ali Termos, and Neil Yorke-Smith, "Initial Results from an Agent-based Simulation of Housing in Urban Beirut, " *The American Association of Medical Audit Specialist* (AAMAS) (2018): 45–47.
17. Sun Shipeng and Steven M. Manson, "Simple Agents, Complex Emergent City: Agent-based Modeling of Intra-urban Migration," in *Computational Approaches for Urban Environments*, eds. Marco Helbich, Jamal Jokar, and Arsanjani Michael Leitner (Cham: Springer, 2015), 123–147.
18. Peter A. Thompson and Eric W. Marchant, "Simulex; Developing New Computer Modelling Techniques for Evaluation, " *Fire Safety Science* 4, no. 6 (1994): 13–24.
19. Zhu Wei, De Wang, and Harry Timmermans, "Applying Multi-agent Systems in the Simulation of Consumer Behavior in Shopping Streets: The Shanghai East Nanjing Road Case," *Acta Geographica Sinica* 64, no. 4 (2009): 445–455.
20. Andrew Crooks et al., "Walk This Way: Improving Pedestrian Agent-based Models Through Scene Activity Analysis," *ISPRS International Journal of Geo-Information* 4, no. 3 (2015): 1,627–1,656.
21. Yan Wei and Yehuda Kalay, "Simulating Human Behavior in Built Environments," in *Computer Aided Architectural Design Futures 2005*, eds. Bob Martens and Andre Brown (Dordrecht: Springer-Verlag, 2005), 301–310.
22. Yang Chunxia and Gu Zhuoxing, "Optimization of Public Space Design Based on Reconstruction of Digital Multi-agent Behavior—Taking the Public Space of the North Bund in Shanghai as an Example," 25th Caddria Conference, no. 1, 2020, 335–345.
23. Huang Weixin and Xu Weiguo, "Urban Morphology Generation Based on Parametric Design Methods," *New Buildings*, no. 1 (2012): 10–15.
24. Li Fang, *Multi-agent-based Emergency Evacuation Model for Subway Platform Passengers* (Beijing Jiaotong University, 2015), 35–96.
25. Hong Seung Wan, Davide Schaumann, and Yehuda Kalay, "Human Behavior Simulation in Architectural Design Projects: An Observational Study in an Academic Course," *Computers, Environment, and Urban Systems*, no. 60 (2016): 1–11.
26. Jane Jacobs, *The Economy of Cities* (Vintage, 2016), 33–35.
27. Peng Zhikai, Yi Wang, and Li Lisha, "Correlational Study on Thermal Comfort and Outdoor Activities," *Journal of Physics: Conference Series* 1,343, no. 1 (2019): 12–25.
28. Liu Yuanyuan and Toshiyuki Kaneda, "Using Agent-based Simulation for Public Space Design Based on The Shanghai Bund Waterfront Crowd Disaster, " *AI EDAM* 34, no. 2 (2020): 176–190.
29. Kostas Cheliotis, "An Agent-based Model of Public Space Use," *Computers, Environment, and Urban Systems 81* (2020): 101,476.
30. Fan Peilei et al., "Accessibility of Public Urban Green Space in an Urban Periphery: The Case Of Shanghai," *Landscape and Urban Planning* 165 (2017): 177–192.
31. Yang Chunxia, et al., "Waterfront as the Public Space of the City-research on the Waterfront Park of the North Bund in Shanghai," *Advanced Materials Research*, vol. 807 (September 2013): 33–36.
32. Nigel Gilbert, *Computational Social Science: Agent-based Social Simulation, Agent-based Modelling and Simulation* (University of Surrey, 2007), 115–134.
33. David Schaumann et al., "Simulating Use Scenarios in Hospitals Using Multi-agent Narratives," *Journal of Building Performance Simulation* 10, no. 5–6 (2017): 636–52.
34 Cheliotis, "An Agent-based Model of Public Space Use, Computers."
35. Jan Gehl et al., "How to Revitalize a City," Project for Public Spaces, February 29, 2008, https://www.pps.org/article/howtorevitalizeacity.
36. Gehl and Gemzøe, *Public Spaces – Public Life.*
37. Michael Batty, Jake DeSyllas, and Elspeth Duxbury, "The Discrete Dynamics of Small-scale Spatial Events: Agent-based Models of Mobility in Carnivals and Street Parades," *International Journal of Geographical Information Science* 17, no. 7 (2003): 673–697.
38. Cheliotis, "An Agent-based Model of Public Space Use, Computers."
39. Batty, DeSyllas, and Duxbury, "The Discrete Dynamics of Small-scale Spatial Events: Agent-based Models of Mobility in Carnivals and Street Parades."
40. Cheliotis, "An Agent-based Model of Public Space Use."
41. Paul M. Torrens, "Intertwining Agents and Environments," *Environmental Earth Sciences* 74, no. 10 (2015): 17–31.

Figure Credits

Figure 1: Situation of public space in the North Bund, Shanghai (authors' drawing).
Figure 2: Statistics on the distribution of public space activities in the North Bund (authors' drawing).
Figure 3: Micro-activity and spatial selection model (authors' drawing).
Figure 4: Simulated space environment construction (authors' drawing).
Figure 5: Spatial sampling grid design (authors' drawing).
Figure 6: Multi-agent behavior flow (authors' drawing).
Figure 7: Simulation of headcount monitoring (authors' drawing).
Figure 8: Activity track record (author's drawing).
Figure 9: Rate of visits to activity points (authors' drawing).
Figure 10: Total activity record (authors' drawing).
Figure 11: Heat map of activity density distribution (authors' drawing).
Figure 12: Activity time distribution heat map (authors' drawing).

Scenes Reconstruction: A Strategy Study of Ethnic Village Revitalization Based on the Activation of Shared Space

LI Minqian, Huazhong University of Science and Technology, China
LI Xiaofeng*, Huazhong University of Science and Technology, China

Abstract

There are many traditional settlements in the Yi Autonomous Prefecture of Chuxiong, Yunnan Province, China. With the decline of traditional industries and the serious loss of population, ethnic villages are rapidly hollowing out, and the value of villages as living communities has been gradually weakened. This paper aims to cognize the interactive relationship between shared space and living forms at all levels in traditional Yi settlements, and to activate the shared space through the strategy of "scenes reconstruction." This paper first analyzes Yi settlements from the aspects of "collective life and ritual scenes," "livelihood mode and production scenes," and "residential units and living scenes." It then proposes specific strategies, including spatial scene design strategies at the village level, group level, and household level, as well as the "mother tongue construction" strategy in the construction process. This study expects to make proposals for rural revitalization and the continuation of collective memory in ethnic villages.

Author Information
LI Minqian: d201880900@hust.edu.cn
LI Xiaofeng (*corresponding author): lixf@hust.edu.cn

Keywords

Scenes reconstruction, the Yi nationality, ethnic village revitalization, activation of shared space, design strategy.

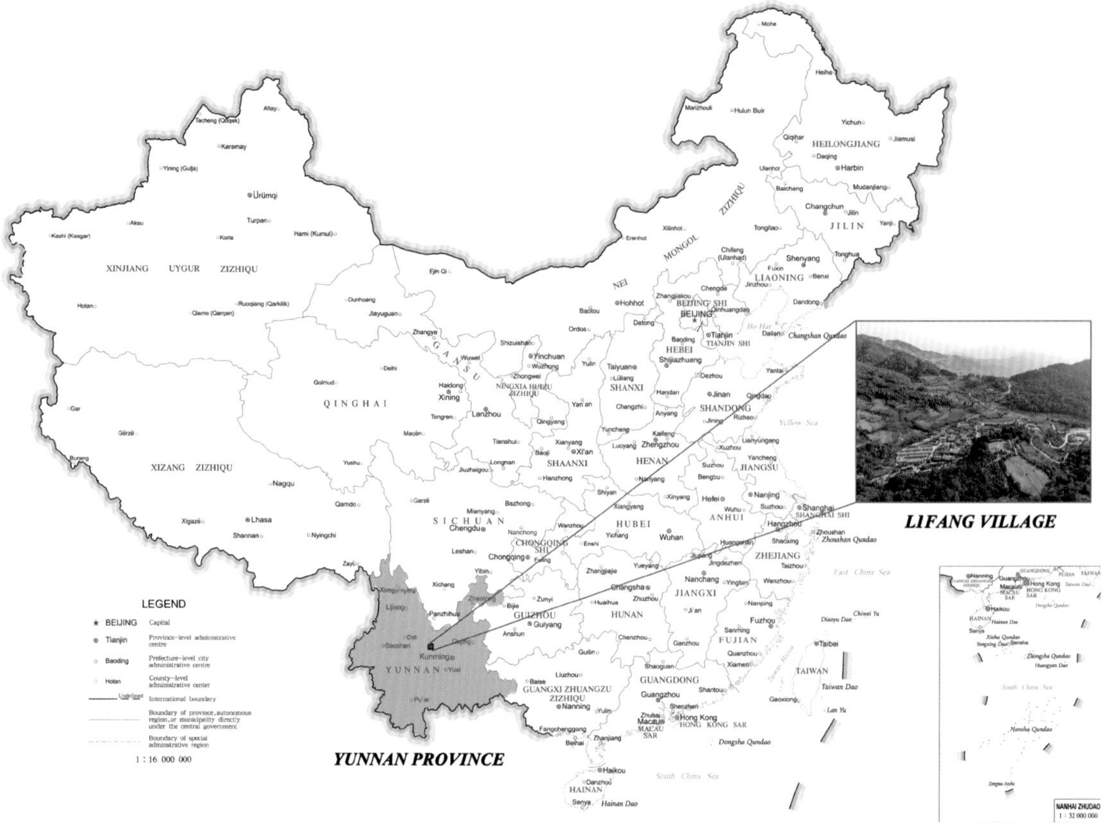

Figure 1
Location of Lifang Village in China

1. Introduction: The Concept of Sharing for Ethnic Village Revitalization

In the sphere of economics, sharing the right to use one's personal idle goods or resources forms the core of the sharing economy, and it aims to explore the potential social and economic value of idle goods and resources.[1] Sharing also makes political sense with regards to social equity.[2] In 2016, the United Nations Habitat III Conference proposed a goal: "A City for All." Four years before that, in 2012, the fifth Plenary Session of the 18th CPC Central Committee had also put forward the concept of shared development. Professor Wang Hui of Tsinghua University, a recognized public intellectual, believes that "Spatial Justice" should be regarded as the premise of "sharing," based on American political philosopher John Rawls' Justice Theory.[3] At the spatial level, philosopher and sociologist Henri Lefebvre believes that "space" is a place where social activities are carried out, which are subject to different interests and different groups. "Sharing" means the organization, union, and use of a space by a crowd. Sharing is not only a way to use space, but also a regeneration of space exchange value. Well-known columnist Li Zhenyu believes that Sharing Architecture includes three forms: the traditional "sharing for all," "sharing by transfer," which is in constant development, and the emerging "group sharing." There are also the four spatial forms of sharing expression: separation, stratification, timing, and differentiation.[4]

Ethnic villages are mostly composed of consanguineous ethnic groups or formed because of a geographical relationship. The people of ethnic villages work and live together, they resist enemies and reproduce offspring as a community, and so sharing is, in fact, an age-old concept for ethnic villages. The need for sharing exists in all aspects of community life, such as sharing production resources, interpersonal relations, and social information. The spatial form of the village directly reflects the concept of sharing. However, this kind of traditional sharing mainly occurs inside the community, which is a type of sharing under the original commune system. In today's context, with the development of various production modes, life needs, and internet technology, the meaning of sharing has changed. For example, the sharing group expands from the inside of the community to the outside world, which includes administrative department, tourists, investors, tourism companies, and so on. Also, the way of sharing has become diversified, given the development of the internet. On the spatial level, some traditional public spaces have become difficult to identify, and some are disappearing.

There are abundant public spaces and public activities in Yi settlements. However, in recent years, with the decline of local traditional industries, there appears a serious loss of population and decline of public life. Ethnic villages are rapidly hollowing out, even moving toward disintegration. The public spaces in villages have gradually shrunk, and the value of villages as community life has weakened.

In recent years, the concept of sharing has been developed in urban renewal. However, the renewal of ethnic villages and urban renewal are faced with different backgrounds and problems, and therefore, strategies and mechanisms for the activation of shared spaces in ethnic villages still need to be explored.

2. The Culture of Yi Settlements and Dwellings

The Yi nationality (a Chinese ethnic group) have a long history and brilliant culture, mainly distributed in Yunnan, Sichuan, Guizhou, and Guangxi provinces of China (Figure 1, page 36). For generations, they worked and thrived in the high mountains and valleys along the southeast margin of the Yunnan-Guizhou plateau and the Kang-Tibet plateau. The Yi people have their own languages, writing system, and calendars. There are many branches of Yi nationality, which are widely distributed, and which form six main dialect clusters. Among them, they share a variety of costumes and customs. Fire is the symbol of the Yi nationality, symbolizing their pursuit of light, and black, red, and yellow are their favorite colors.

Chuxiong Yi Autonomous Prefecture is located in the central and northern parts of Yunnan Province, the central Yunnan region to the south of Jinsha River, and the transition zone between Hengduan Mountains and the Yunnan-Guizhou plateau. The mountainous area of the prefecture accounts for about 90 percent of the total area. The substantial difference in the terrain creates an obvious vertical climate difference that spans across seven climatic zones, moving from low to high. Yi nationality settlements are scattered in the mountains and the communities have developed various residence types to adapt to different climate and terrain conditions. These include: Tuzhang dwellings (土掌房), one of the oldest types of traditional houses of the Yi nationality, where the building material is mainly clay and the roof is flat, wooden houses, and tile-roof houses. Tuzhang dwelling villages are mostly built in line with the mountain, forming a highly identifiable cultural landscape. People can walk around the whole village via the roof of the houses, with the help of stairs and slabs. The village has no obvious center and the connected roof space is the main shared space in the village. Wooden house villages are mostly distributed near the flat dam or at the foot of the mountain, forming a courtyard-type layout. Generally, public houses or squares in villages are used as the center to form architectural clusters of different sizes.

3. Traditional Collective Life and Public Spaces in Yi Settlements

3.1 Collective Living and Ritual Scenes

A settlement, in essence, means to live together. The public space system of a Yi village represents the way of their collective life. In a Yi settlement, the village gate, bridge, alley, central square, temple, and bullring form a multilayered shared space. The ritual space in a Yi village is usually divided into an etiquette and custom space, and a sacred ritual space. The etiquette and custom space refers to the house, courtyard dam, temporary youth shed, the open space at the entrance of the village, known as *cunkou* in Chinese, and the village gate used by people in marriages and funerals. The sacred ritual space refers to the ancestors' "soul caves" and the sacrificial field used for ritual ceremonies of ancestor worship.

There are also lots of public buildings in Yi settlements, such as youth sheds, which are temporary buildings that are meant to be easily demolished, constructed on the basis of the original shanty of the nomadic period. In today's modern times, Yi people use this architectural form for weddings, festivals, and funerals. Another public structure is the public house, which is specially built for unmarried young boys and girls to court within Yi settlements. All unmarried girls live together in the public house, and unmarried boys are welcome to come in and profess their love to them and court them, almost like a place for them to group date. These are jointly built by all residents and are usually the oldest and largest building in the village. These days, the old marriage customs have been abandoned and the public house has become a place for young people to exchange production skills and engage in entertainment activities.

Figure 2
Residential units and living scenes

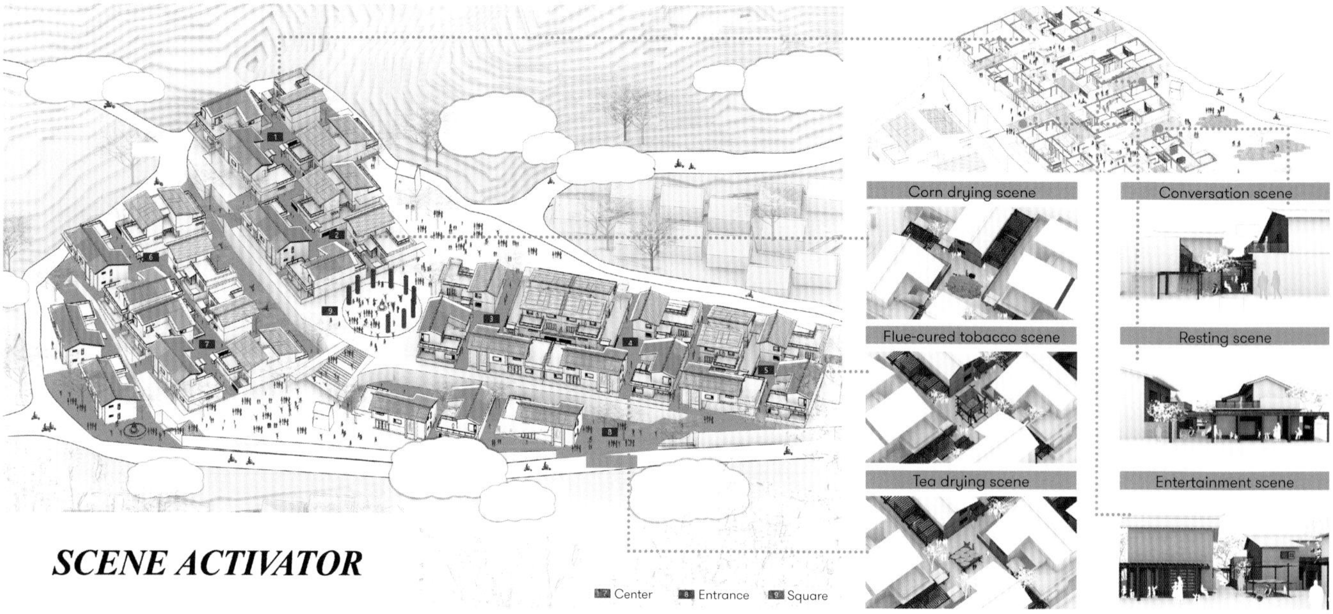

Figure 3
Scene activator

Many types of ritual activities of the Yi people closely link the collective together and make up the people's self-identity and collective memory. These ritual activities connect the public spaces at all levels of the village through the people's practices and daily routines, and also represent the social structure and life order inside the settlement. One example is the Jump Tiger Festival held annually in January, where the Tiger God "descends" to earth and walks with the procession from the Tiger God temple to people's homes, and then leaves the village through the "evocation bridge" (a mythical bridge that leads spirits "home"). This route symbolizes the space transition of God space–human space–ghost space, which reflects the space hierarchy in a village.

3.2 Livelihood Mode and Production Scenes

The village's mode of livelihood and mainstay industry have a profound impact on the settlement form of Yi settlements, where many public spaces are often included in the layout for production tasks. Chuxiong's Yi nationality's traditional livelihood mainstays include corn, flue-cured tobacco, and tea. They also create folk craft, such as silverware, lacquer ware, embroidery, and paintings, among other handicrafts. Under the influence of the traditional farming economy, the form of Yi settlements is often determined by the distribution of land resources for cultivation, forest land resources, and water resources. In order to save the limited land resources for cultivation in mountainous areas, houses are often built on sloping land and grow in a vertical direction.

In the past, barns were often located in the safest area of the villages, in accordance with fire and rodent prevention requirements. In the development process of farming villages, courtyards have emerged in the form of housing, in order to adapt to agricultural production, due to the increasing demand for grain storage, grain drying space, rice processing sites, and production tools storage. Industrial development also promotes the development of village public space and public buildings. The collective activities in the farming economy, such as rice processing and construction of grain drying facilities promoted the emergence of fixed public spaces in Yi settlements in the dam area. These public spaces are generally located on relatively flat site in the center of the settlement and have gradually assumed functions that include goods trading, religious sacrifice, public communication, and transportation hubs, and at times even evolved into open market places.

The Yi people also make full use of the "in-air" platform function of the flat-roofed Tuzhang dwelling villages. In areas with complex terrain, there is no flat and spacious land to form a square, so rooftops or attached platforms are generally used as spaces for outdoor activities. Some villages connect the roof platforms in a variety of series to become entertainment venues for women to do handicrafts, children to play, and youth to sing and dance.

3.3 Residential Units and Living Scenes

The basic structure that establishes Yi societies is the clan organization, made up by blood relations known as the family branch system, and which forms a tight clan network and denotes the custom of the family division system. In the early period, the living units of Yi settlements were divided into numerous small families from large families and the houses were built with small families as the unit, forming relatively independent production and living units spanning specific functional areas around the families (Figure 2, page 37).

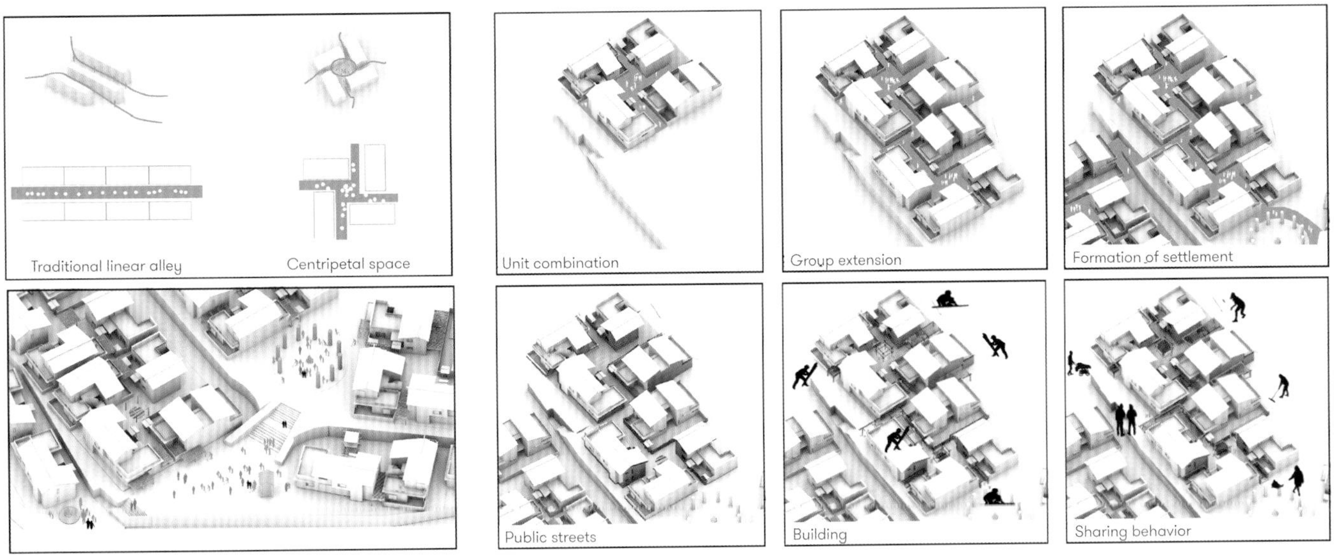

Figure 4
The growth process of units

Under the influence of the central pillar worship, a typical Yi residence presents the vertical division of storage, residence, and livestock, symbolizing the separation of God, human, and ghost space. In terms of plane space function, the single sacred space of a Yi residence is set in the lobby room, which is the venue for guests, weddings, and funerals. In the middle of the hall, ancestors and Gods are enshrined. The hall is not only for human use, but also regarded as God's residence, which is the space for people to communicate with their almighty and ancestors. Although the traditional fire pit (or *huo-tang*) of Yi nationality is not in the center of the space, it is the core of daily family life. "Fire ponds" have the function of cooking and roasting bacon. In humid mountainous areas, fire ponds play the role of drying, keeping warm, and repelling insects. The daily routine of Yi people would usually be to light a fire in the morning and then spend the rest of the day around it. From eating, resting, chatting, and entertaining guests, this habit has not changed through the times. Because of its importance in family life, the fire pond space is endowed with sacred significance. The three stones in the fire pond have special names and represent different sacred positions. At the same time, the seating order around the fire pond also represents the hierarchy of the family inside and outside the home, and also denotes the order of the elder and younger members. This seating order also defines the sleeping space of different family members, as well as the organizational structure of the family.

The Yi family life extends from indoors to outdoors. The *shazi* refers to the space under the front eaves of the sloped roof that stretches out in front of the house. This space can not only block rain but also provide shade from the sun. It is the transitional space between inside and outside, the space for Yi women to embroider and do work, and the place for family members to gather and chat or exchange a drop of gossip. The courtyard and yard dam outside a Yi residence are also important places for families to carry out daily tasks. Also, if there is a girl within the household above the average marrying age, she would choose a room as a "daughter room," so that she may fall in love and be wed.

4. Scenes Reconstruction: Strategies in Activation of Yi Settlements

The concept of the "scene" originally came from film art, which includes dialogue, setting, props, music, costumes, and actors to convey the message and feelings that the film seeks to impart to the audience. In the scene, the relationship of each element is usually organically related to each other. Terry Clark, professor of sociology at the University of Chicago, introduced this concept into the study of urban society, and then formed the scene theory of urban sociology, and constructed the analytical framework of the quantitative study of the urban scene. In the field of anthropology, architecture is regarded as a scene—a state and scene in which people interact with the environment. Architectural anthropology believes that architecture is not only a spatial form or a system form, but also a process and result of certain events. Architect Chang Qing believes that the task of architecture is not only to shape the space and satisfy the function. If architecture is regarded as an organizational form, it should not only conform to the function, but also to the current customs, behavioral habits, and scene atmosphere, and also the pleasure of physical contact.[5] In addition, professor Li Xiaofeng and Li Ting from Huazhong University of Science and Technology believe that the spatial scene contains the dual contents of physical space entity

Figure 5
Residential workshop unit

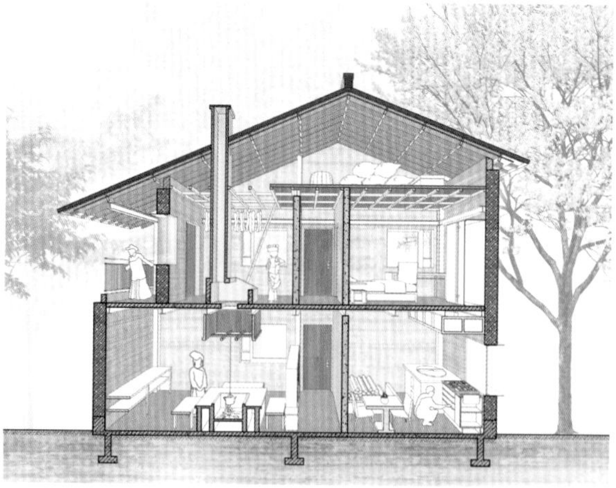

Figure 6
Profile of residential building

and immaterial behavior events. The coupling of spatial elements and behavior events, and the mutual weaving of physical architecture and spiritual memory is conducive to the development and inheritance of local culture.[6] The scene reconstruction strategy of ethnic villages is based on the background of village public life, coupling the public space at all levels with crowd behavior, taking the scene as the clue and sharing as the concept, to integrate the village space into a shared space.

This study examines Lifang Village in the Yi Autonomous Prefecture in Chuxiong. Located in Baizhu mountain, a provincial scenic spot, Lifang Village is the birthplace of Daluosheng (大锣笙), a primitive totem dance of sacrifice and entertainment inherited from the ancient Yi tribes. The agriculture in Lifang Village is mainly corn and flue-cured tobacco, among other crop varieties. In the future, focus on the development of flue-cured tobacco, corn, walnut, animal husbandry, and agricultural products processing will create new ecological agriculture demonstration villages. Lifang Village retains distinctive national culture, including the Dagongsheng culture, and the Bi Mo (village shaman) culture, and strengthens its heritage through events and folk crafts that include the Torch Festival, Dragon Festival, folk embroidery, and folk songs. The main public activity spaces are Gong Sheng Square, Fire Square, and Earth God Temple. The public space in the village is small and there are few places for villagers to chat after dinner. Typical dwellings in Lifang Village consist of tile-roof houses left over after 1949.

The natural texture of local villages and their protection are relatively intact. Typical mountain villages form a good vertical landscape, which is integrated into nature. Given such a design, any architectural update to a village should respect and protect the regional characteristics of local buildings, and the characteristic mountain landscape should be created according to the existing terrain.

4.1 Spatial Scene: Activation of Shared Space

4.1.1 Village Level—Scene Activator

The public spaces of this traditional village are the plane-shaped Lu Sheng field, Fire Festival square, the courtyard dam, and the small open spaces at the front and back of the houses. The public spaces also include linear traffic and walking areas along the river bank and the point-shaped wellhead, and the space under trees. The Yi people have the custom of "sacrificing the dragon" during the annual Dragon Festival. It is usually held on the first day of the first lunar month. The activities usually last three days and are centered around "sacrificing the dragon," "inviting the dragon," "turning the dragon," and "jumping the dragon." The Lifang Village Torch Festival is held from the 23rd to 29th of the sixth lunar month. People gather in the village square to dance around the fire and organize a carnival to worship the God of Fire.

At the village level, the design tries to reintegrate the public space existing in traditional culture, which is broken and slowly disappearing under the impact of modernization; it also aims to combine the concept of sharing to give it new significance, to adapt it to modern developments and current-day routines. The youth shed in traditional Yi dwellings is usually a bamboo and wood structure that has the flexibility to be easily built and removed, and is usually constructed from bamboo, wood, and thatch commonly found in the local mountains. When not in use, it can be removed and stored away or used for other living needs, which conforms to the villagers'

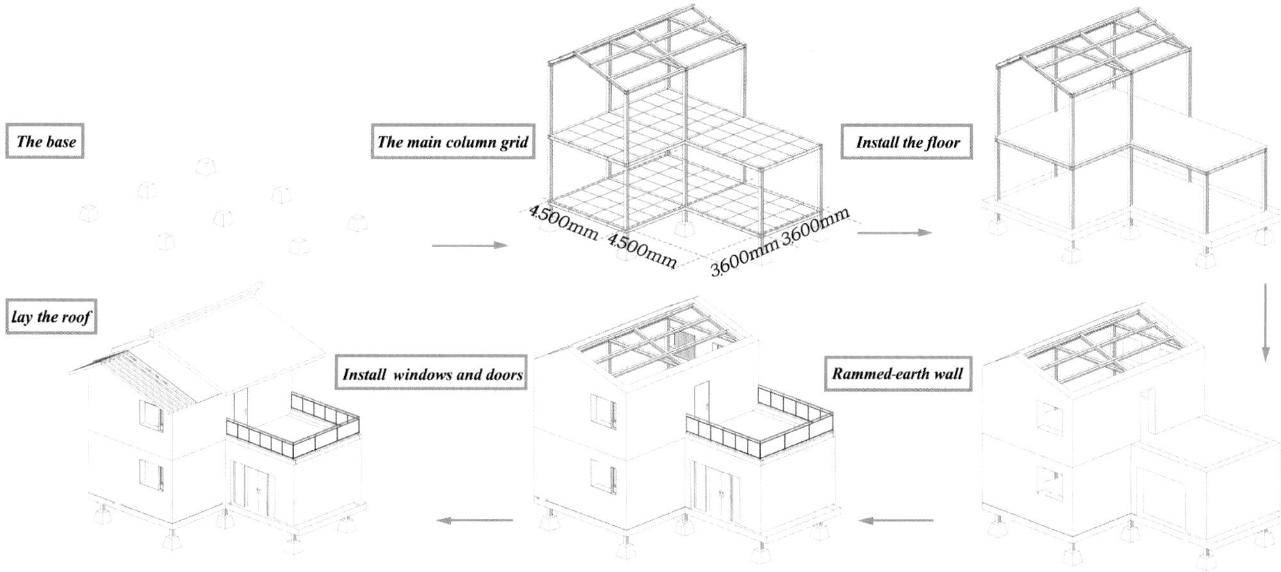

Figure 7
Building program

economic considerations and concepts shaped toward environmental protection. Youth sheds were used in the past for weddings, funerals, Tiao Cai ceremonies, and other occasions, where temporary outdoor venues were needed to ensure that residents' outdoor activities could be carried out conveniently in sheltered spaces without disruption from the elements.

Based on the traditional youth shed construction concept, this study designs a set of unitary outdoor structure systems referred to as a "scene activator" (Figure 3, page 38). Also made from wood and bamboo, the modular design forms a series of small units that can be copied and spliced to adapt to different scales of space. These small units can provide shade for pedestrians, serve as places to stay or rest, act as support for planting climbing plants, and overall function like a group of public furniture in the village, providing spaces for people's outdoor tasks and entertainment activities, so as to accommodate the scene activities at the public level of the village. At the same time, the system is designed to stimulate the encounter and communication of different groups of people and activate more sharing behaviors (Figure 4, page 39).

4.1.2 Group Level—Residential Workshop Unit

With regards to the residential cluster mode, the isolation caused by the single linear space is changed, and the centripetal enclosing layout is adopted. Every group of four residential houses forms a point-like central space, and every two houses forms a linear space. Thus, the cluster continues to grow and expand, and point space and linear space continue to extend into systematic public space in the settlement. The generated system and continued public spaces are the scene activators in our design strategy. These design strategies aim to stimulate production and life scenes.

The direction of the industrial development of Lifang Village is based on agriculture, which demand open "drying" sites. In addition, Lifang Village has inherited an outstanding intangible cultural heritage that includes curing ham, tea making, crafting festival masks, wine making, and Yi embroidery. A Yi nationality residence is a complex mix of production activities and life. Lifang Village intends to combine the existing characteristics of catering and non-material culture to create a household, and also develope farm homestays and a farming industry.

The design combines living and production activities and business households, grouping four households to form a residential workshop unit (Figure 5, page 40). The group is centered on the collective activity site, which can be used as a site for the residential courtyard to extend to the outside world, and shared by the residents within the group. It can not only serve as an auxiliary space for production activities, but also form a good community atmosphere, embracing relationships of mutual assistance. Residential workshop units can make use of any idle space and rent it to migrant populations in need, and also give full play to the value of a surplus labor force of rural "left-behind" populations, and form a self-sufficiency mode at home.

4.1.3 Household Level—Translation of Traditional Culture and Democratic Design

At the household level, four categories of units are designed for different family compositions and different space requirements. They are: a 114-square-meter unit for a family of three, a 152-square-meter unit for a family of four to five people, a 232-square-meter unit for a family of five to six people, and a 275-square-meter unit for a family of six to seven people or more. In terms of functional composition, these apartments continue the important spiritual space and living space segregations of traditional Yi dwellings, but also make adjustments according to the new needs of contemporary life. The disadvantages of poor lighting and ventilation that existed in traditional residential houses, as well as the lack of separation between human and livestock spaces have been altered. The new plan preserves the core position of the hall, continuing the axisymmetrical layout centered on the shrine, while incorporating modern comfortable and convenient furniture. The design also retains the fire pond room in a modern update (Figure 6, page 40).

The plan also designs two or three small courtyards with different functions for each household, so as to separate people from livestock and meet the needs of farmers for spaces to dry produce. In terms of roof design, the combination of the flat roof with the slope-roof not only continues the roof characteristics of traditional Yi dwellings, but also increases the functional space of the flat roof. Variable spaces are also incporporated to support the concept of sharing and to meet the needs of farmers to create handicrafts or develop tourism functions like homestays. This part of the space can be used for storage or other auxiliary space functions for leisure, or even redesigned into a snack shop, handicraft production room, or a Yi history exhibition hall.

The building adopts a steel structure main body and improved rammed-earth masonry walls (Figure 7, page 41). To extend the excellent thermal performance of rammed-earth, natural lighting and warmth is increased by way of windows. Through the translation of traditional dwelling features and cultural symbols, the architectural form continues the traditional architectural nuances of the Yi nationality, such as the traditional roof, window frame decoration, and mountain wall decoration.

4.2 Construction Scene: Mother Tongue Construction

4.2.1 The Continuation of Traditional Building Organizations

The traditional construction system of Yi nationality relies on the village community. Designers, builders, and homeowners all come from within the community. They are familiar with each other and even have a high degree of overlap in identity. The Bi Mo (毕摩) of the Yi nationality is a shaman who plays a ceremonial (not technical) role in construction activities. Tasks from the selection of materials—determined through a sacrificial ceremony—to site selection, orientation, interior space division, and other religious rituals are completed by the Bi Mo. The construction team is mainly composed of carpenters, bricklayers, stonemasons, and so on, led by the chief wood craftsperson. Building activities within the community exist in mutually beneficial community relations and are related to the secrets of community life. In the new design, we encourage the continuation of skills of the traditional craftspeople in the village, the use of traditional technology, and co-construction and sharing within the community (Figure 8).

4.2.2 The Inheritance of Traditional Construction Skills

As an important intangible cultural heritage, the skills of craftspeople are of great significance to the continuation of the characteristics of ethnic villages. However, in recent years, there has been a serious aging curve among traditional craftspeople, as well as generational crisis issues. Compared with static material space, it is more effective to continue traditional skills. Craftspeople make their living by reputation, and since everyone in the community knows each other, skilled and ethical craftspeople naturally gain a good reputation and receive work. As a secret of their trade, their skills are often usually passed down verbally and

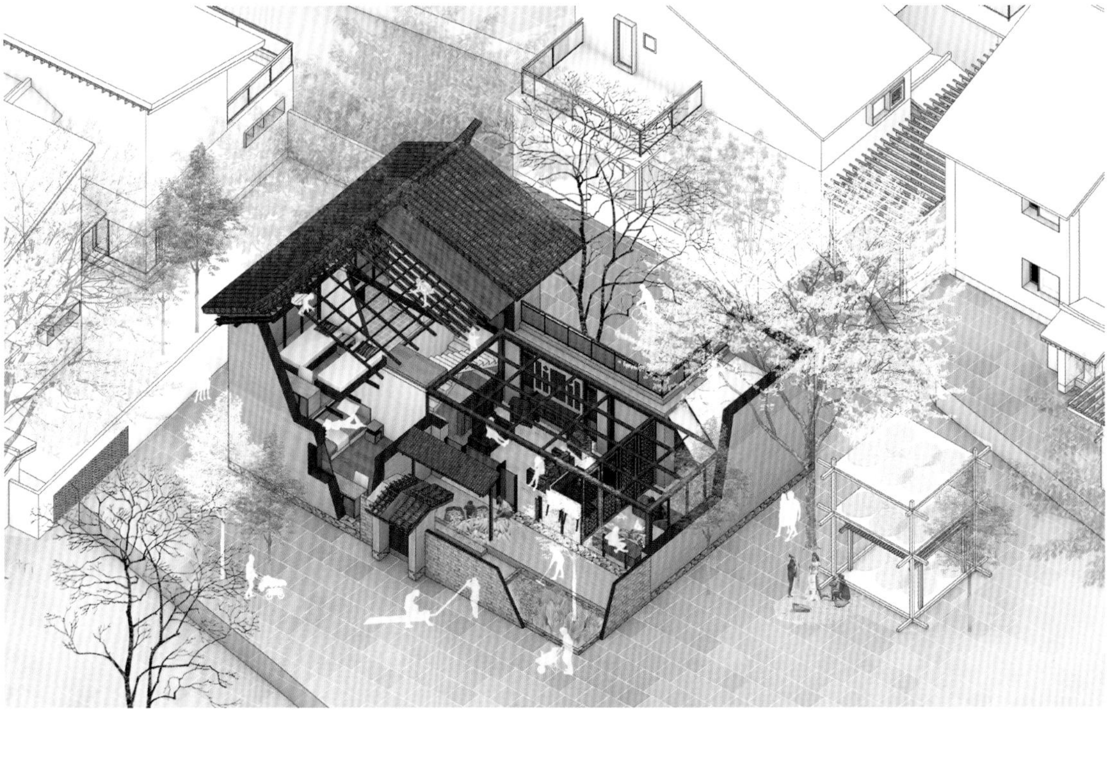

Figure 8
Construction under the concept of sharing

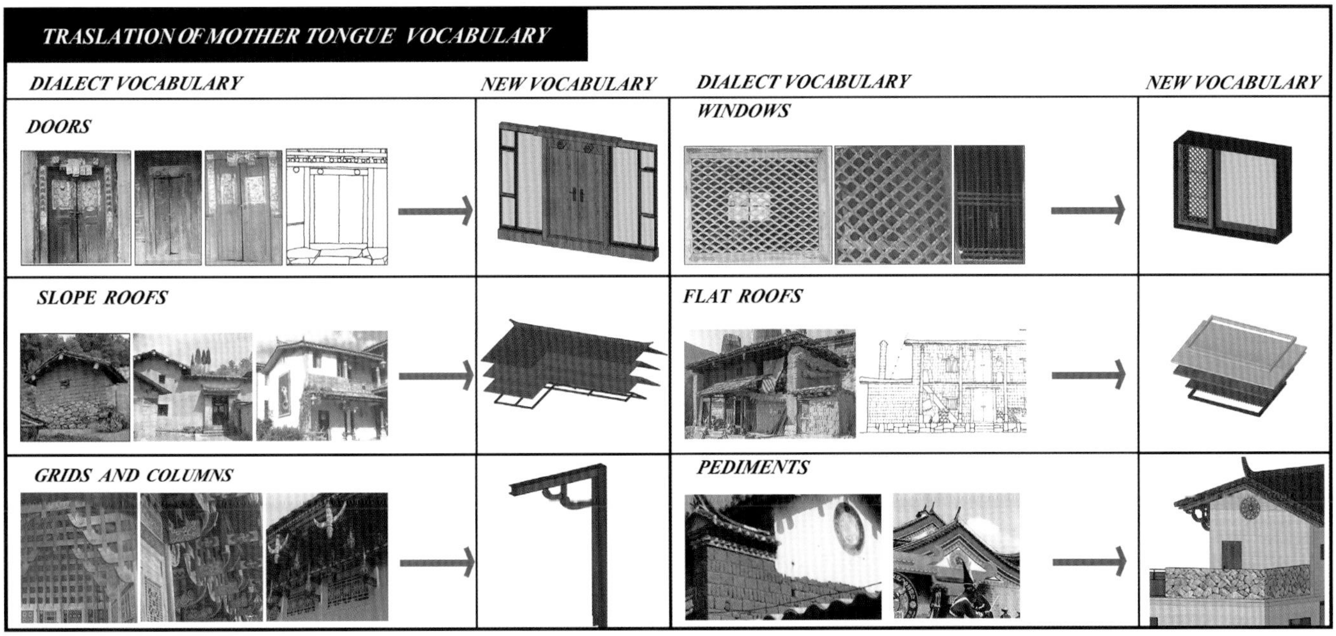

Figure 9
Mother tongue vocabulary

through observation and teaching. Unfortunately, this affects the inheritance and spread of these skills. Under the concept of sharing, training institutions for craftspeople should be established as soon as possible, to encourage the younger generation to pass their skills on. The sorting of dying-out traditional skills should also be accelerated, so as to form a database, in order to form a wider range of information sharing (Figure 9).

4.2.3 Information, Technology, Materials—Sharing beyond Community
Against the national background of rural revitalization, and with the support of the internet, the collaboration, participation, and common interests of ethnic villages today usher in more opportunities. A sharing trading platform for rural areas can be established to productize idle rural resources into products that consumers can share directly, such as private kitchens in farms, homestay facilities with time rights, agricultural experience, and purchase of agricultural products from other places, so as to maximize resource demand matching. Through the sharing of information, new technologies, and new materials, we can build villages together to move toward producing the very resource itself.

5. Conclusion

This paper discussed the design strategies of the revival of ethnic villages under the concept of sharing. The concept of "sharing behavior" is an ancient concept in ethnic communities, but its meaning has changed in contemporary life. The research puts forth the public space sharing concept with a modern take to successfully activate these spaces to serve their full potential. The concept of sharing has also been developed in urban research and will make great developments in rural construction in the future.

Acknowledgments

This paper is supported by the National Natural Science Foundation of China (Grant No. 51978297) and is based on the team's design results; hereby, thanks is extended to the advisor Li Xiaofeng, and team members Wu Shuhuan and Wang Yanbo. Thanks is also extended for the support of the People's Government of Chuxiong Yi Autonomous Prefecture, Yunnan Provincial Department of Housing and Urban-Rural Development, and *New Architecture Magazine*.

Notes
1. Liu Genrong, "Shared Economy: The Subversion of the Traditional Economic Model," *Economist*, issue 5, 2017, 97–104.
2. Shi Nan, "Sharing," *City Planning Review* 07 (2018): 1.
3. Wang Hui, "Space Sharing from the Perspective of Spatial Justice: Using Rawl's Justice Theory to Investigate the Hutong Renovation Projects by URBANUS," *Time + Architecture* 04 (2021): 80–85.
4. Li Zhenyu and Zhu Yichen, "Towards a Sharing Architecture," *Architectural Journal 12* (2017): 60–65.
5. Chang Qing, "An Anthropological Perspective on Architecture," *The Architect 06* (2008): 95–101.
6. Li Ting, Li Xiaofeng, and Guan Ruiming, "The Study on the Spatial Scene of Sibao Ancient Printing Workshop in Western Fujian," *New Architecture* 06 (2018): 42–47.

Figure Credits
Figure 1: Location of Lifang Village in China, 2021 (based on the standard map of China, http://211.159.153.75/browse.html?picId=%224o28b0625501ad13015501ad2bfc0264%22; drawn by authors).
Figure 2: Residential units and living scenes (authors' drawing).
Figure 3: Scene activator (authors' drawing).
Figure 4: The growth process of units (authors' drawing).
Figure 5: Residential workshop unit (authors' drawing).
Figure 6: Profile of residential building (authors' drawing).
Figure 7: Building program (authors' drawing).
Figure 8: Construction under the concept of sharing (authors' drawing).
Figure 9: Mother tongue vocabulary (authors' drawing).

MoMA

This extraordinary design and randomness in the streetscape provide another way of thinking about Asian architecture

Architect firm: HAS design and research
Principal architect: Jenchieh Hung, Kulthida Songkittipakdee
Design team: HAS design and research, TROP: Terrains + Open Space, Light Is
Location: Nonthaburi, Thailand
Area: 400 square meters
Completion date: January 2022
Photography: W Workspace

The Museum of Modern Aluminum (MoMA) project came about because of a group of ambitious clients who sought to revive the significance of aluminum in Thailand. Thailand was once the largest aluminum manufacturer in Southeast Asia at the end of the twentieth century. Its diverse and abundant aluminum profiles not only satisfied the local market, but were also exported to overseas markets. However, in 1997, the Asian Financial Crisis hit without warning, forcing Thailand's aluminum industry to sell aluminum at low prices to hardware markets around the country. This, in turn, created a clutter of advertising signs, balcony fences, and ground-floor extensions that make up the present-day Bangkok streetscape.

MoMA is born out of such an environment. It is located at the busiest traffic hub on the outskirts of Bangkok, where heavy traffic has led to a variety of commercial marketing signs lining Ratchaphruek Road, in the hopes of catching the eye of motorists. The main roads lead to The Grand Palace, Wongwian Yai, Bangkok University, and to Ko Kret, the only island in Bangkok. More than a decade ago, fireflies populated Ko Kret, making the island a natural retreat for Bangkokians.

The design team wanted MoMA to serve not only as a public space, but also as a getaway for busy urban dwellers. The building extends the natural landscape of Ko Kret Island to the project site. During the day, MoMA is a dandelion, with its overhanging elements swaying in the wind, bringing softness and lightness to the busy Ratchaphruek Road; at night, it transforms into a firefly, adding a sense of nature and peacefulness to the street.

The design process began with the study of aluminum signboards commonly seen on the streets, and then used aluminum as an element to link the entire building. MoMA not only uses aluminum strips as display items, but also allows them to continue in the architecture, the interior, the landscape, as well as in the lighting and furniture, creating a sense of totality inside and outside. The façade is clad with tens of thousands of aluminum strips, each with a slightly different color and texture, just like the wispy, feathery petals of the dandelion. The aluminum strips, combined with LED lighting, extend from the front façade to the two side façades, and then straight through the "tunnel" space on the west side, filtering and dampening the noise of the external environment as they guide visitors to the quiet exhibition space.

On the façade, they not only provide a variety of lighting functions, but also shade the interior from excessive sunlight to maintain a comfortable interior environment. The flexibility of the exhibition space can meet a variety of display, reception, and activity needs. On the top floor, the enclosed landscape resembles a floating island with seasonal plants, creating an urban ecological site for fireflies to flourish. Through the investigation and research of aluminum profiles, a distinct architectural texture is created, and a new sense of vernacular is established in Thailand's concrete jungle.

The "tunnel" gallery space is a mediator between the interior and exterior

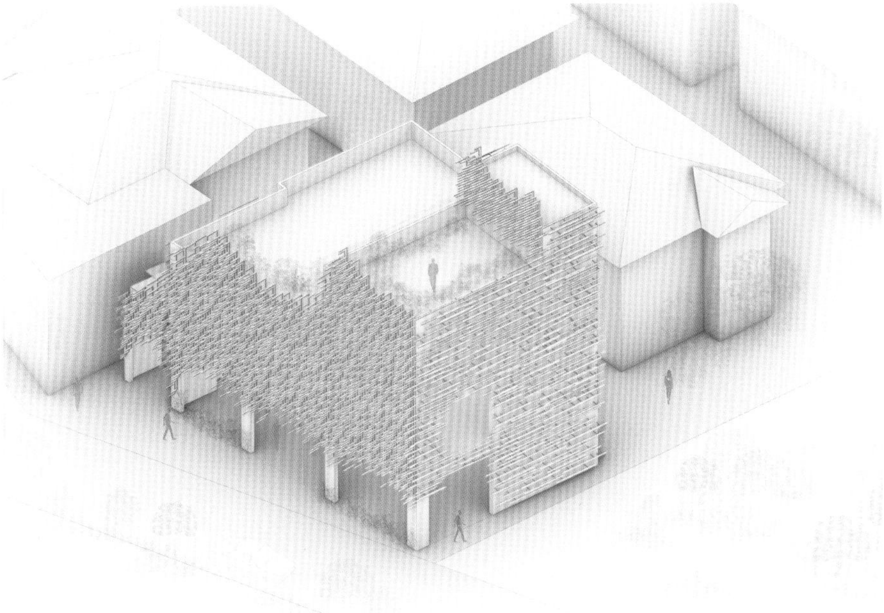
Isometric diagram

An aerial view shows the site's surroundings and the overall look of the architecture

The impressive outdoor space connects the façade elements to the furniture

View from the exhibition space toward the outside

The consistency between the side and front façade elements generates continuity in the experience

The “tunnel” creates a unique arrival experience, filtering noise out to quiet the mind

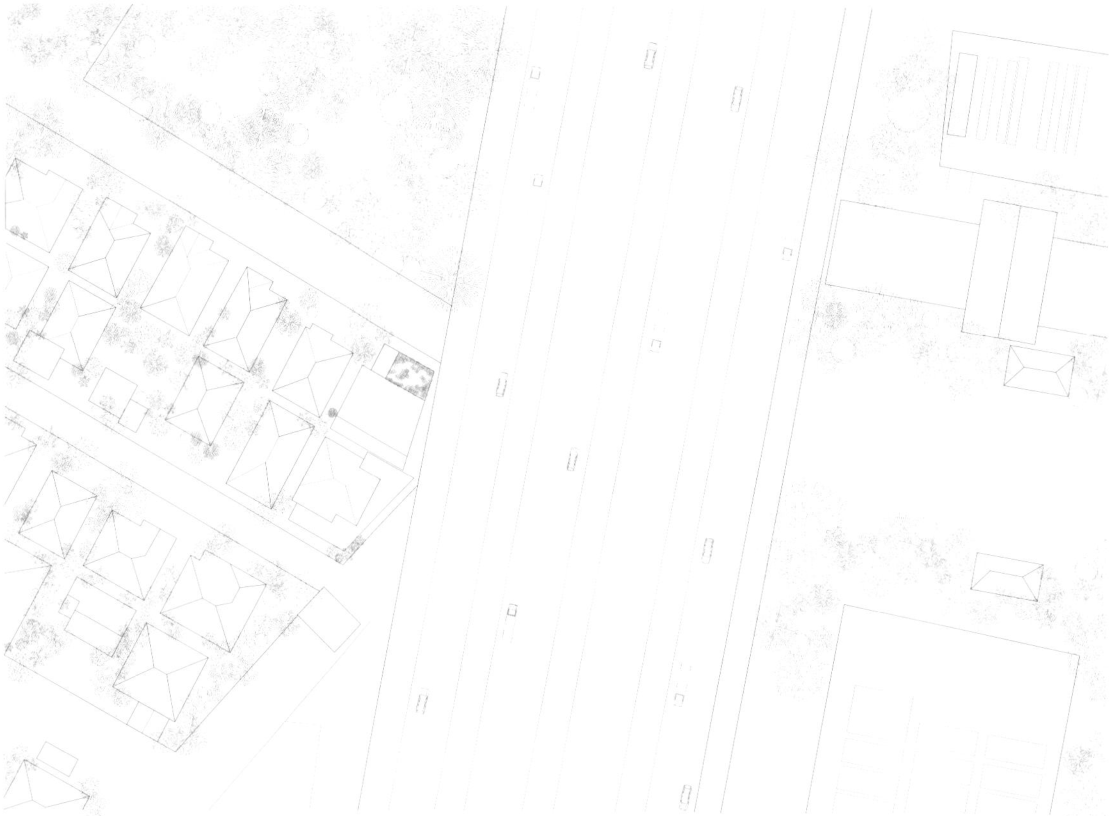

Roof plan

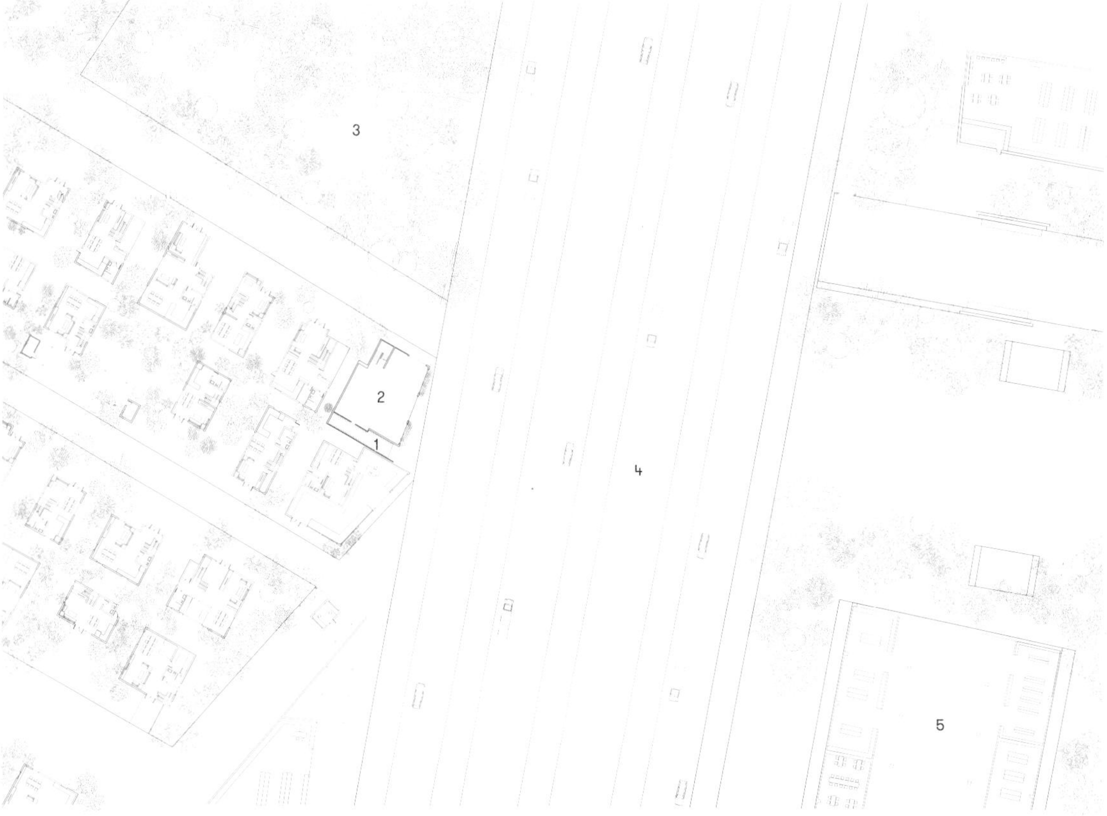

Ground-floor plan

1. Tunnel gallery
2. Multifunction exhibition hall
3. Green area
4. 52-meter-wide road
5. Mall

MoMA creates an eye-catching standout image along a major road

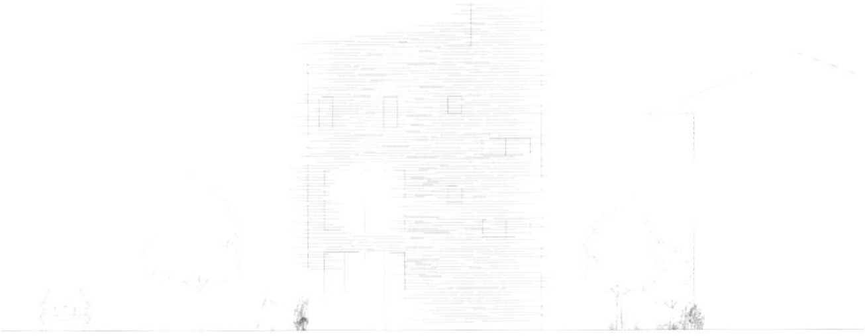

North elevation

South elevation

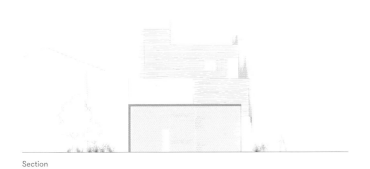

Section

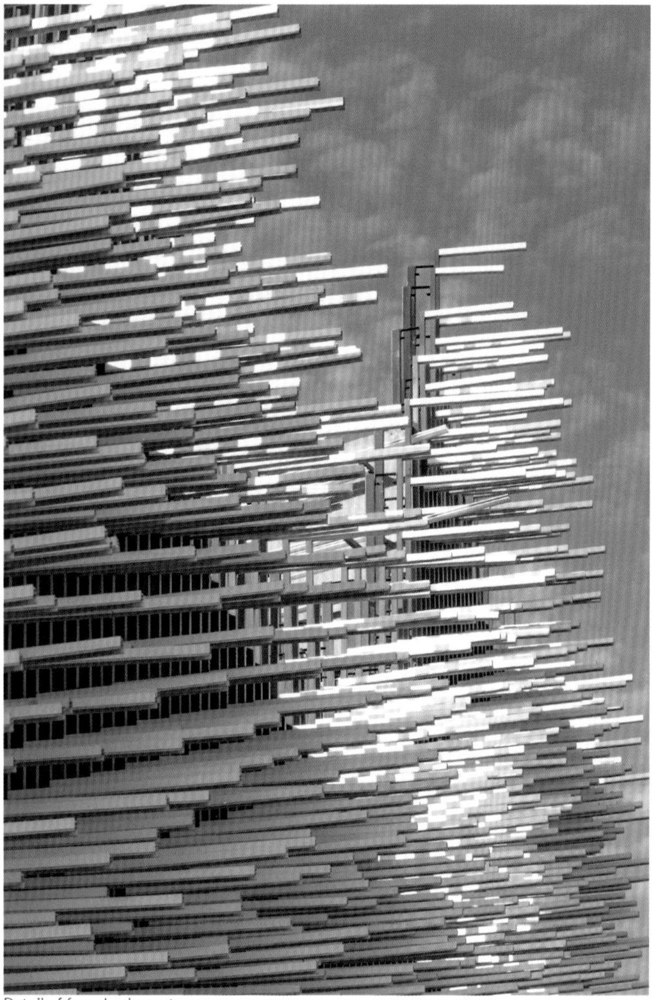

Detail of façade elements

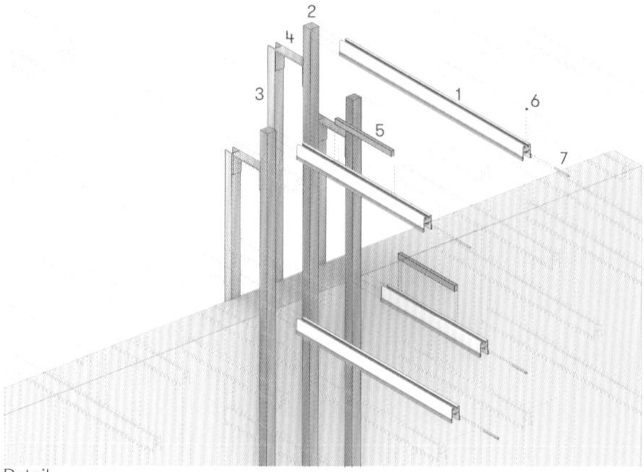

Detail

1. Aluminum profiles (length: 350, 450, 550, and 650 mm)
2. Aluminum structure (25×25 mm)
3. C steel structure
4. C steel bracket
5. Led strip light
6. Led dot light
7. Hidden screw

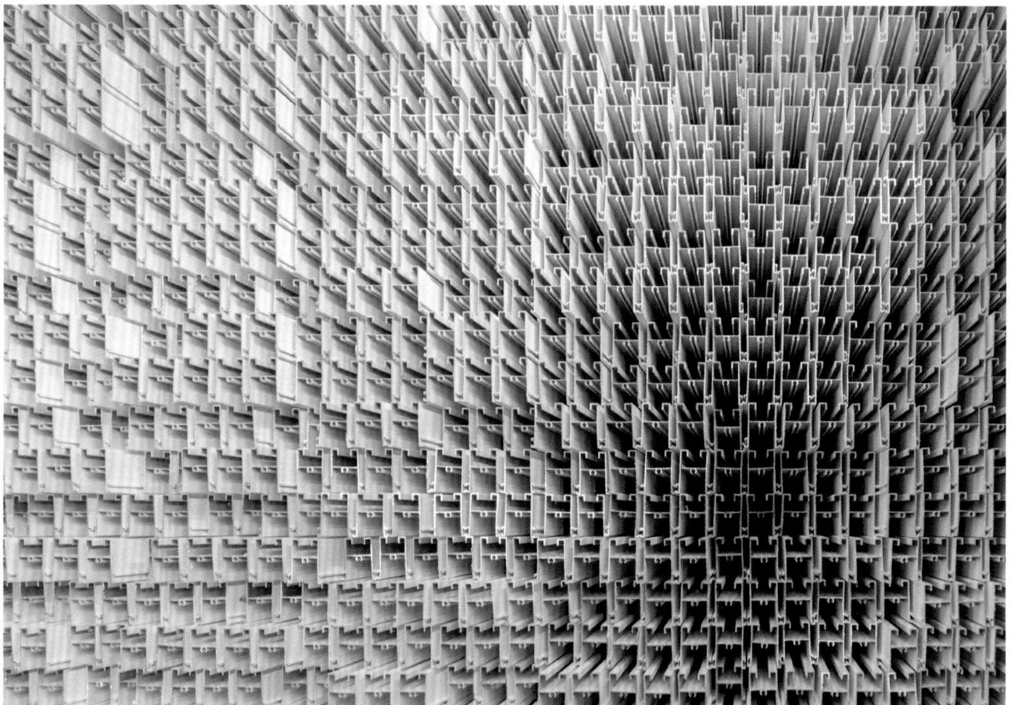

The aluminum profiles arrange a dynamic wall

Office Complex for Gopal Printpack Solutions

View of the entire complex from the main entrance

Architect firm: I-con Architects and Urban Planners
Principal architect: Dhaval Rangani
Design team: Vishal Akabari, Chetna Shethiya
Location: Rajkot, India
Area: 494 square meters
Completion date: October 2019
Photography: Bhavesh Raghavani, Yellow-Frames Photography

Gopal Printpack Solutions is one of the leading companies in Gujarat delivering customized packaging solutions. The factory is located in Metoda, an industrial zone in Rajkot. The office building is designed to be the most representative element, while the factory acts as a backdrop. It is a square-plan structure that is deliberately tilted at an angle against the rectangular site and factory, so that it stands out on the site.

The intention was to develop a design language that showcases the typical manufacturing process that takes place in the factory, where a blank plastic sheet is dipped sequentially into inks of various colors, so they amalgamate to form the final Printpack. This idea of amalgamation is abstracted and expressed through the landscape and the façades. The factory façade is clad in Corten steel, chosen for its inherent property to withstand weathering, resulting in an amalgamation of changing colors, which is representative of the client's manufacturing process. This façade acts as the backdrop to the entire complex, while the foreground features extensive landscaping that seamlessly integrates with the office building. The core façades of the office building constitute tilted concrete walls that act as a skin, wrapping around the building.

The curvilinear steps in the landscape act as an amphitheater and spill into the congregation space. This space directly connects to the factory and is tucked away from the sightline of the main entrance to allow privacy. The arched walls at the periphery are structural elements that bear the entire load, creating diffused light that makes the space an intimate gathering area for factory employees. The extensive landscaping situates ramps that lead to the office building, allowing staff to slow down and meander along the landscape; seating is also incorporated, so factory employees may enjoy a comfortable and calming space among nature to take a break from the industrial work environment.

A stone pathway leads to the entry bay of the office building, which stands out invitingly against the blank façades of the structure. As one enters the building, one arrives in the waiting area facing the courtyard. The greenery in the courtyard extends the outdoors and offers the respite of nature within the office building. The workstation, private cabins, and meeting room are organized around this space. Although physically segregated to justify the efficiency of function, these spaces are visually connected to the owner's cabin, which is suspended from the roof, thereby transcending the restrictions of closed office habitats. The suspended cabin connects to the factory with a bridge that overlooks the manufacturing process on one end, while leading to the dining area and guest hosting rooms on the other. This bridge allows the owner to share an overview of the factory to clients without disturbing the manufacturing process.

Along with exposed concrete and metal, raw wood is also used in various areas to impart warmth and tactility to the space. A skylight that runs around the core of the structure and the tilted walls situates triangular openings among them that create a play of light and shadow on the raw concrete walls, while keeping the spaces well-lit throughout the day.

View of the bridge connecting the office building to the factory

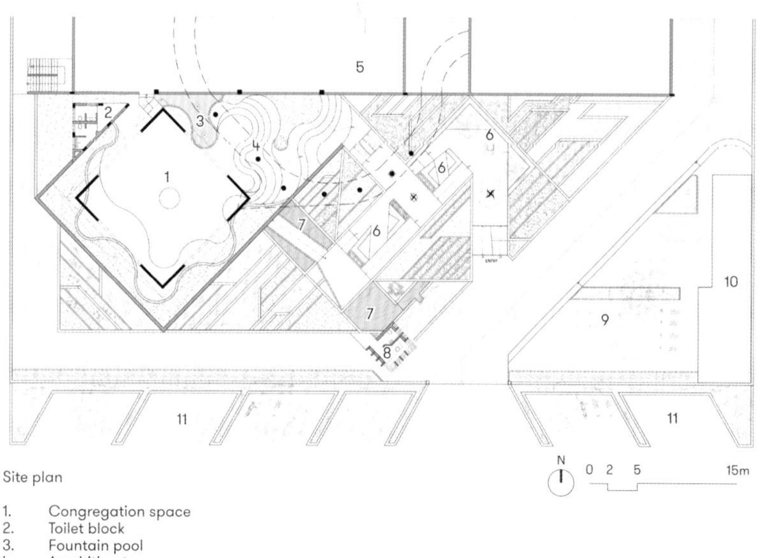

Site plan

1. Congregation space
2. Toilet block
3. Fountain pool
4. Amphitheater
5. Factory
6. Seating space
7. Waterbody
8. Security cabin
9. Parking
10. Electrical services
11. Guest parking

Entrance

View of the amphitheater

Congregation space on the lower ground floor

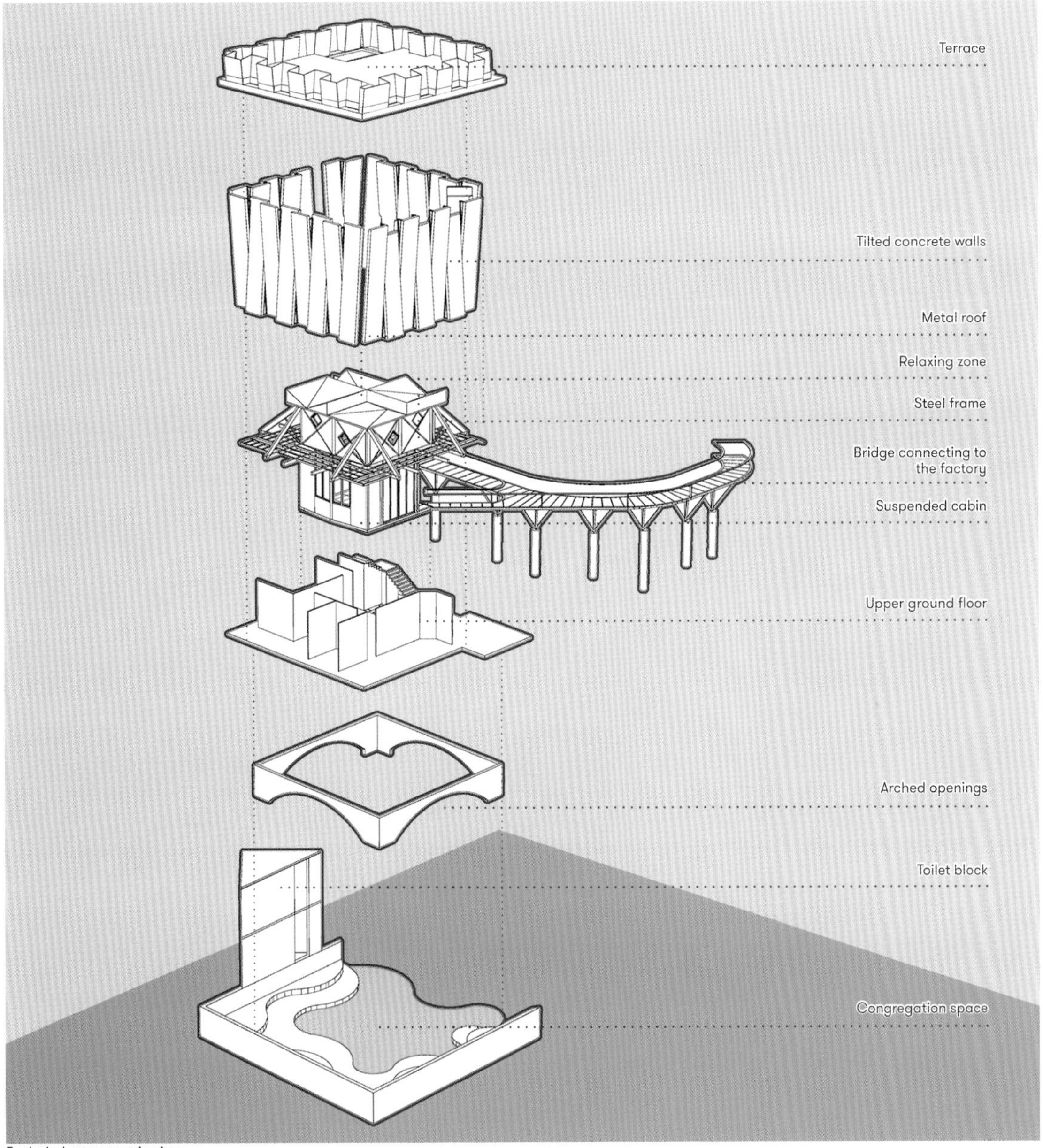

Exploded axonometric view

View of the waiting area and courtyard in the office building

View showing spatial volumes lit by skylight above

Triangular openings and a skylight allow the meeting room to be well-lit with natural light

View of the courtyard from above

The play of light on the raw concrete walls against the backdrop of the landscape in the courtyard creates a sensory experience

Wood cladding in the owner's cabin imparts warmth and luxury

View of the workstation being visually connected with the owner's cabin that is suspended from the roof

The owner's cabin is suspended, overlooking spaces on the lower floor

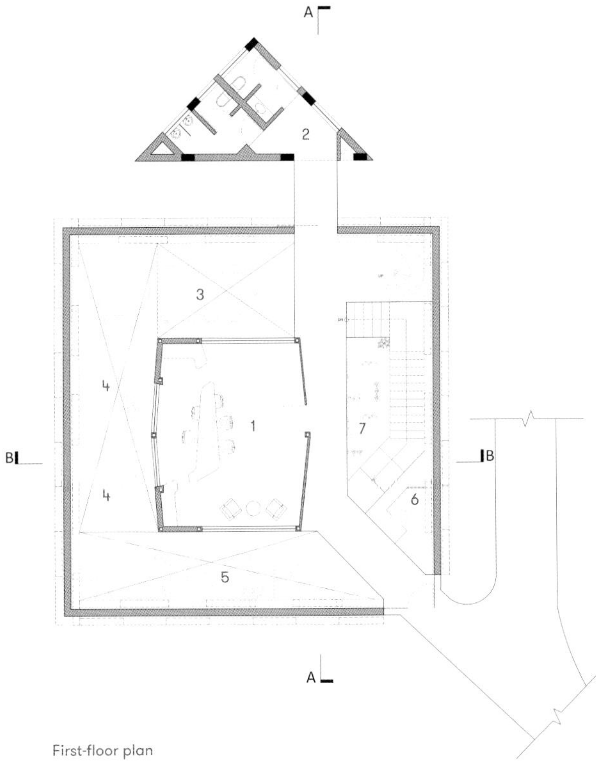

First-floor plan

1. Suspended cabin
2. Toilet block
3. Meeting room below
4. Private cabins below
5. Workstation below
6. Reception below
7. Courtyard

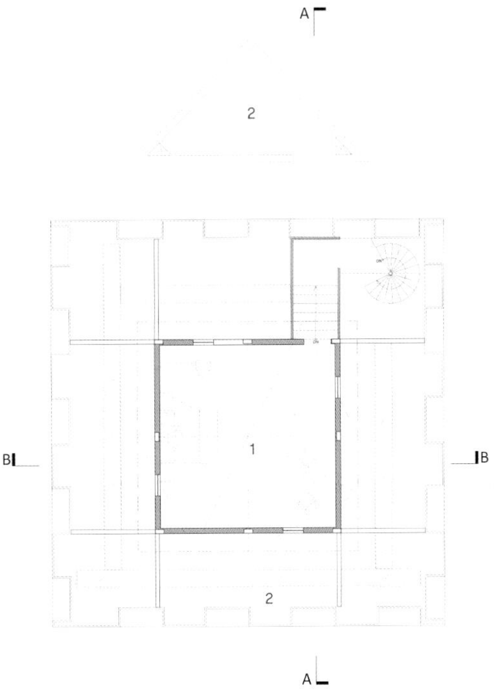

Second-floor plan

1. Relaxing zone
2. Terrace

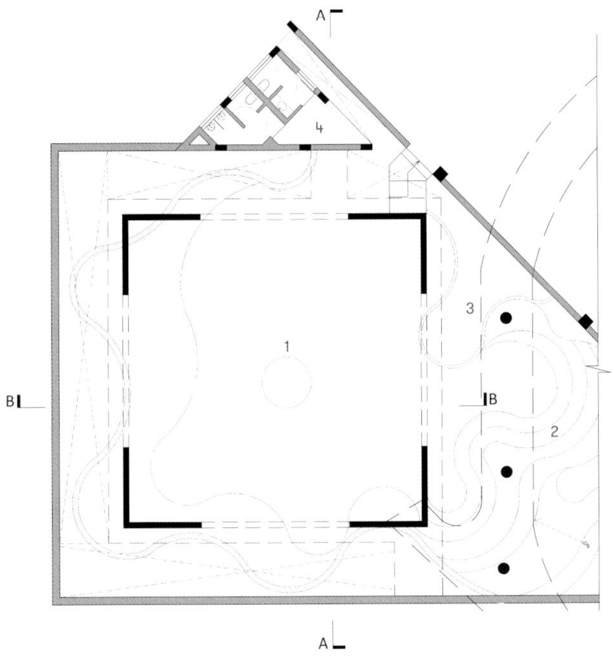

Lower-ground-floor plan

1. Congregation space
2. Amphitheater
3. Lower-level meeting room
4. Toilet block

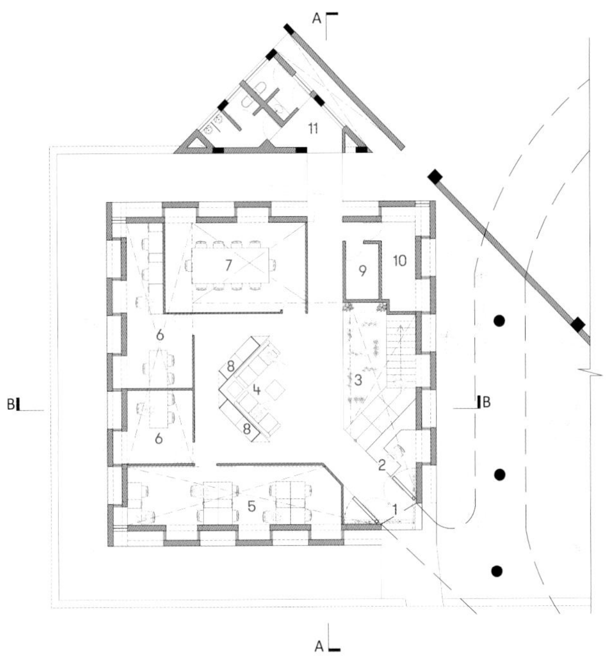

Upper-ground-floor plan

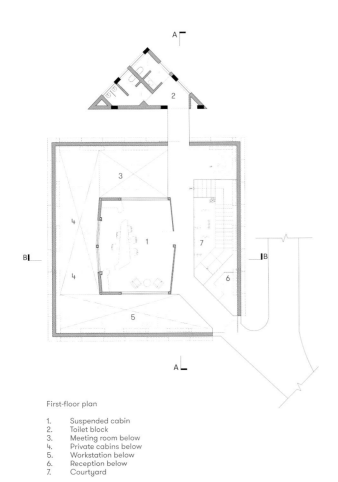

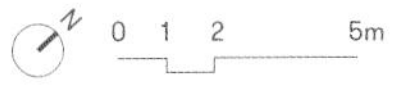

1. Entrance
2. Reception
3. Courtyard
4. Waiting area
5. Workstation
6. Personal cabin
7. Meeting room
8. Storage
9. Server room
10. Pantry
11. Toilet block

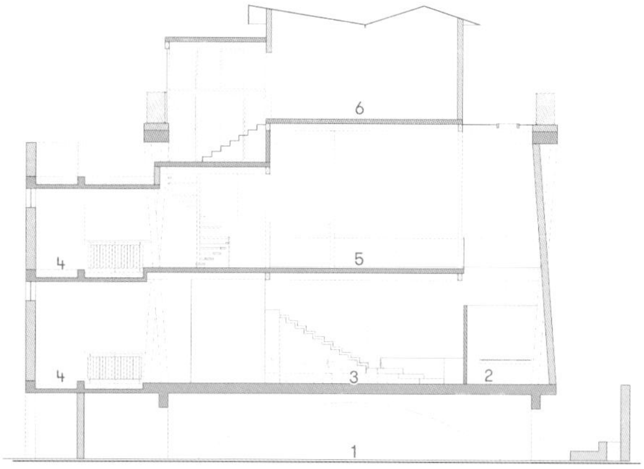

Section AA

1. Congregation space
2. Workstation
3. Waiting area
4. Toilet block
5. Corridor
6. Resting space

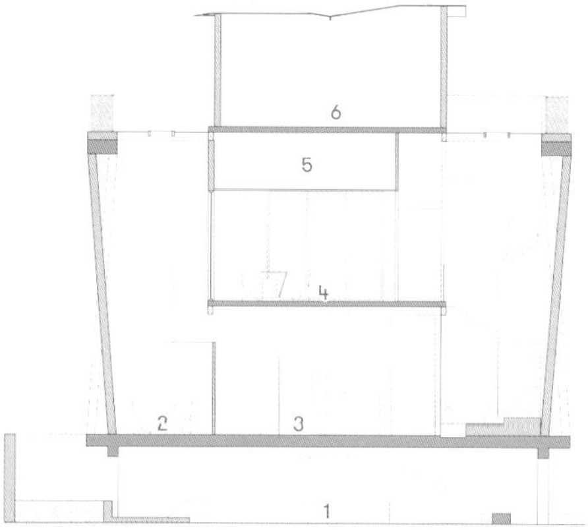

Section BB

1. Congregation space
2. Private cabin
3. Waiting area
4. Suspended cabin
5. Air-conditioning duct
6. Resting space

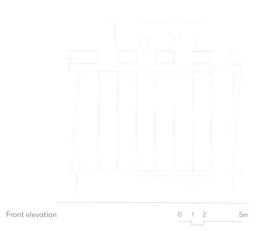

Front elevation

0 1 2 5m

Exterior corner view showing the tilted exposed concrete walls of the office building

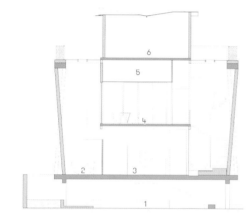

Lushan Times

View from the street

Architect firm: GOA (Group of Architects)
Principal architect: He Jian, Han Zhongqiang
Design team: Wang Haiying, Ye Fan, Gu Jiangchan, Li Zihuan, Hu Jiajia, Xiang Pei, Shi Jianwei, Gong Ming, Shen Xukai, Jin Xiaodong, Ao Guosheng, Shou Guang, Cheng Lei, Jiang Yibo, Zheng Ming, Chen Mengjie, Li Cheng, Mei Yulong, Mao Dihua, Ping Junhui, Hua Yonggang, Li Xiang
Location: Hangzhou, China
Area: 173,000 square meters
Completion date: December 2020
Photography: CreatAR Images

Façade details

The Lushan Times project was launched in 2012 and the building was slated to be a large city-level complex, standing at the gateway of Lushan New Town, which represents the southwest expansion of Fuyang District, Hangzhou. Before taking on this project, the design team had been involved in other projects situated in neighboring areas. Having been continuously working on projects within a certain area, the team began to shift focus from simply looking at individual buildings to considering the interaction of different architecture on a city scale. This led to Lushan Times becoming an epitome of GOA's work in Fuyang.

A Place to See and to Be Seen

The site has a superior location, with Lushan Mountain at the back, and a commanding view of Fuchun River. On one side of the site is Fuyang Bridge, and on the other, is the cultural highland of the new city, Fuyang Cultural Complex, one of Wang Shu's work. From a selected point of view, the building will be the only visible artifact in this landscape. It will present the urban civilization in a certain attitude and become a part of the scroll of this landscape.

The relationship between seeing and being seen is the primary concern in the design concept. On the one hand, the architectural form seen from the opposite bank and the bridge needs to be conceived; on the other hand, the value of the river view, seen from the building, should be fully attained. In line with this, the initial sketch arranged the building along the periphery, forming a square inside to accommodate people activities, while creating a relatively complete volume on the outside. Extended from this idea, the final complex is a double-ring structure, with a sunken circular square nested in the outer curved triangular contour. In between are terraced open spaces with inward-facing retail boxes and small courtyards at different corners. The complete volume of the complex is fragmentized by multiple entryways in all directions, and towers are interconnected through either podium structures or the sky corridor.

The sea is broad, the river is narrow and long. As far as the river view is concerned, its winding nature contributes to views from a variety of angles, making it a unique experience. In this light, the strategy of integration at the periphery not only ensures the purity of the image, but also realizes the maximization and diversification of the river view. In the design process to deepen the building shape, the design team planned with the spatial line of sight in each direction as the standard, successfully achieving both a formal beauty and the value of the line of sight.

Public Spaces: The Stimulus for Urban Vitality

Creating a truly vibrant urban public space is a core issue in the construction of Lushan Times. High-quality public spaces can be important containers of people's collective life and the generator of the city's vitality. This is especially true for Lushan New Town in Fuyang, where public space is still lacking.

As the first urban complex of the new city, Lushan Times, together with the adjacent Fuyang Cultural Complex, naturally defines the "heartland" of people's activities in the new city; they play an important role in shaping the public space of the new city. The architects, therefore, proposed the idea of the "city parlor," which focuses on strengthening the "converging effect" of space, so that the limited building volume and the content of public activities can play a more significant contribution at the city level.

The commercial section in the lower part is designed in a layered stereoscopic outdoor terrace, gradually bringing the ground attributes to the top. It also creates views of the river from multiple elevations, so that the view changes as you walk. The boundary line on the side facing the river recedes to form a concave city square, while the northeast corner facing the nearby cultural cluster is treated with a receding platform to create a friendlier boundary.

The 60-meter-wide void opens a huge "window" for the buildings at the back to view the river, and guides the flow of people in the commercial section. The hotel lobby in the sky corridor becomes a viewing destination with its ultimate river view experience. The value exploration of functional spaces in the upper and lower parts help the complex form "real vitality" under the function synergy.

For large comprehensive buildings, there is often a huge gap between the macro conception and the proper building construction that needs to be addressed by specific strategies. To create a pure, full, and complete form, reasonable strategies are needed to resolve the sense of pressure emanated from large buildings. To do this, the relationship between seeing and being seen is revisited and the design further describes the image of the building from the perspectives of the bridge and the opposite bank. The final façade uses horizontal lines with a variation of thickness to build the rhythm of the curved surface. When viewed from different distances, the horizontal aluminum alloy components, with radians on the curved surface, take on light and shade effects under the light, recalling mountain contours.

Curved surfaces in architecture always present challenges and even small deviations may result in big errors. In Lushan Times, a "gathering parts into a whole" approach is adopted, with a single center leading all the curves, enabling all façades to be achieved by standard unit splicing. This formula guarantees the accuracy of the design scheme in project implementation.

A New Starting Point

At the beginning of the design of Lushan Times, the adjacent Fuyang Cultural Complex had not been built yet. During the design process, the architects simulated the views of the two buildings from different distances, so as to deliberate on the curved form of the buildings along the street, and to review what would be the ideal urban interface from the perspective of the building cluster in the new city. The completed buildings, juxtaposed and in contrast on the waterfront, annotate the new city in different ways.

The conception of Lushan Times in function, activity space, and views brings a brand-new experience to the residents of Fuyang, underscoring the team's objective of looking at the project in terms of the whole city. In the actualization of the project, the holistic consideration of the urban interface became a valuable experience for the team, which also guaranteed the successful implementation of the project conception. The future of this urban complex has only just begun.

View across the river

Aerial view of night scene

1. Building A
2. Building B
3. Building C
4. Building D
5. Building E

Master plan

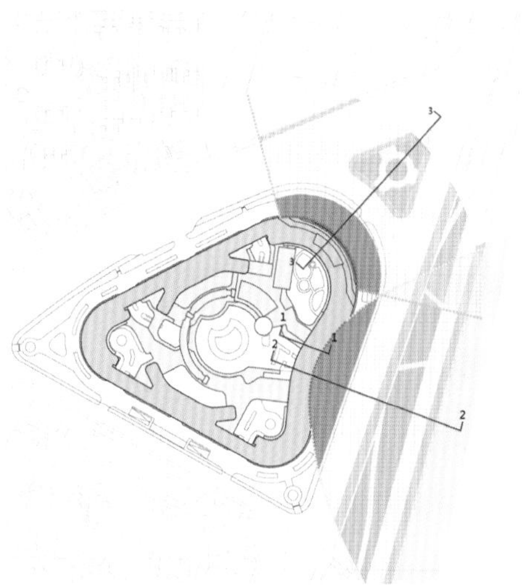

Analysis of main landscape views

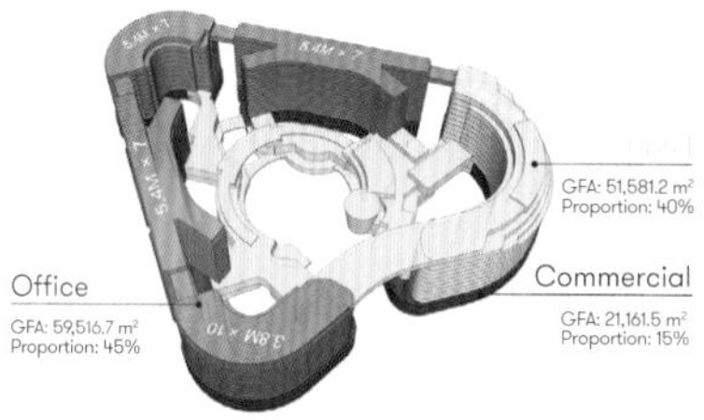

Functional division

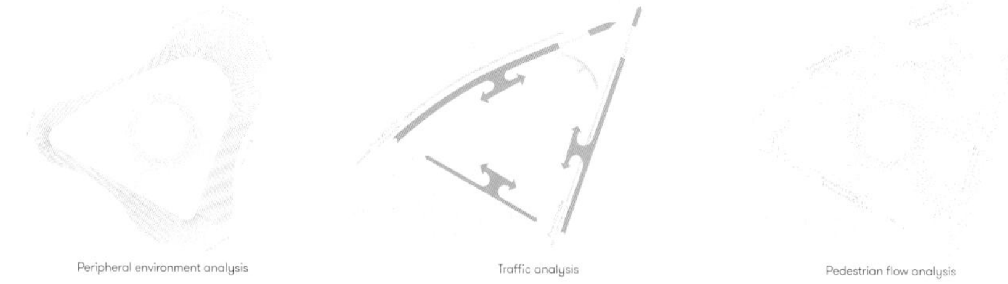

Traffic-pedestrian-scenery analysis

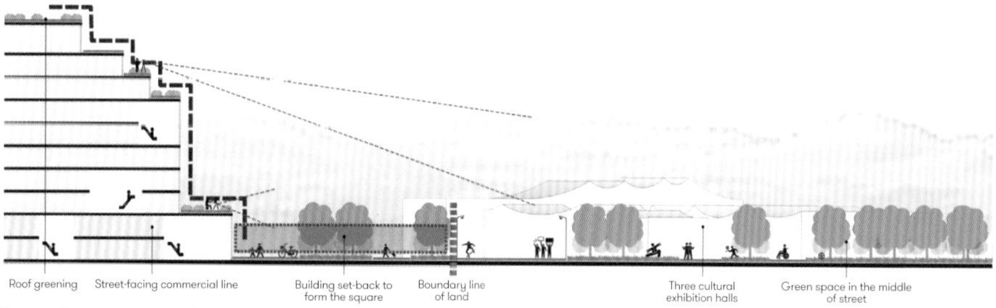

Layered terraces on northeast side

The void structure

Lushan Times building in the city

Night scene: view from the street

Retail businesses are arranged around the sunken square with an open layout

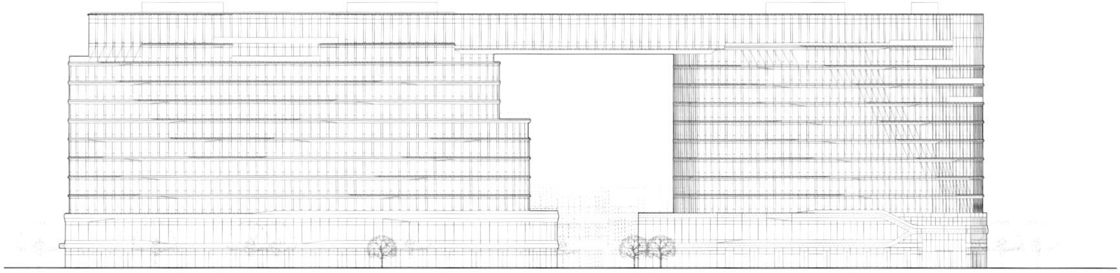

East elevation of Buildings E & A

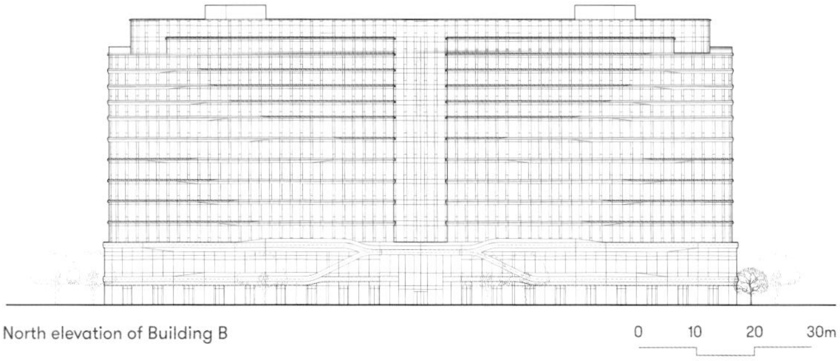

North elevation of Building B

View from the street

Maly Koncert

Approach

Architect firm: Ryo Otsuka Architects
Principal architect: Ryo Otsuka
Design team: Tetsuya Tanaka (Tetsuya Tanaka Structural Engineers), Keiji Oguchi, Ryuichi Wada (Nagata Acoustics)
Location: Tokyo, Japan
Area: 199.04 square meters
Completion date: April 2021
Photography: Keiko Chiba / Nacasa & Partners

The site is located at the end of an arcade that leads from a quiet residential and shopping district in Itabashi-Ku, Tokyo. The surrounding area is very nostalgic, with many houses and small shops, and in springtime, the Shakujii River is filled with people who flock there to admire the pink blooms of the Sakura trees. The architecture's shape is formed by the shape of the site and merged into the neighborhood, standing quietly in the back alley.

When planning a small membership-based music salon in such an area, it is important to ensure that the sound quality is the same as that in a large-scale music hall, and set a high noise control to protect against noise filtering in from the dense surrounding neighborhood. Natural circulation is created with the irregular flagpole-shaped site, entering the space from the rod-shaped part of the site to flow into the rest of it. An attached room is lifted to integrate various functions, which includes storing sound equipment.

In the planning stage, the architect considered the following question: "What kind of space would one prefer, to listen to classical music in?" The answer turned out to be simple, creating a space with enhanced sound effect, where music, musician, and space unite to be one.

A musical instrument in itself has a unique beauty that is reflected in the meticulous craftmanship of its form, the glossy veneer of its finish, and the clarity of its tone. Combined with the performer's showmanship style, the pairing becomes immaculate. To highlight this "total" performance, the space is constructed with powerful raw materials that create a natural focal point on the musicians and their performance. The goal is to craft an instrument-like space that intensifies over time; a modern classic architecture that never pales or stales.

In the main music salon, the proportion of the space is designed based on acoustic simulation, to ensure that sound can evenly reverberate throughout the space within the limited building height. Often, flutter echoes occur when the ceiling, floor, and wall are arranged parallel to one another. To avoid this, numerous acoustic panels are added to ensure that the sound can spread evenly throughout the space. The plan and site are shaped as an irregular quadrilateral, and a square roof is adopted for the double-height section. This achieves a uniform acoustic effect, while also making practical sense for equipment to be displayed under the sloped ceiling.

The main space is designed to be pillar-free, with reinforced-concrete walls, to secure and contain the echo of base tones. The design makes good use of the linear space in the small site, improving overall noise control, as well as incorporating necessary equipment and buffer zones. The space is proportioned in a mix of hardness and softness—hardness from the architecture, and softness from the sound effect, giving the space a balanced harmony.

Staircase

Radiant cooling and heating system

Entrance hall

Music salon

View from the corridor

Music salon

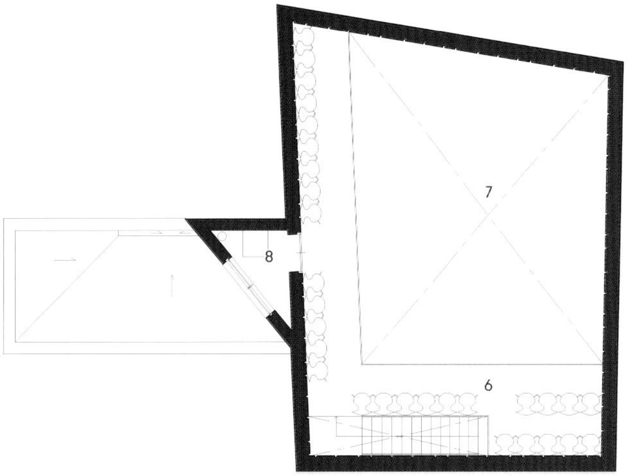

Third-floor plan

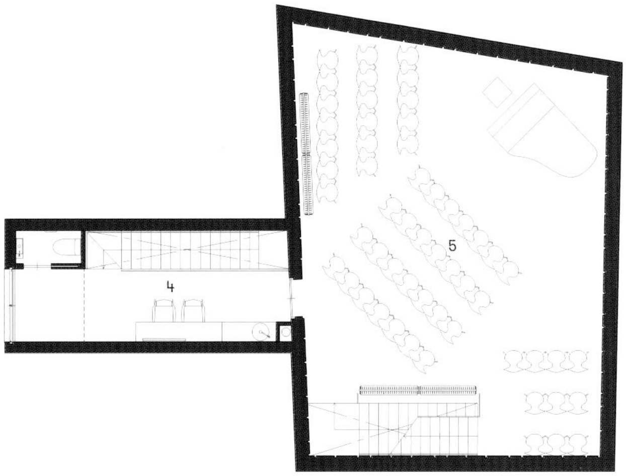

Second-floor plan

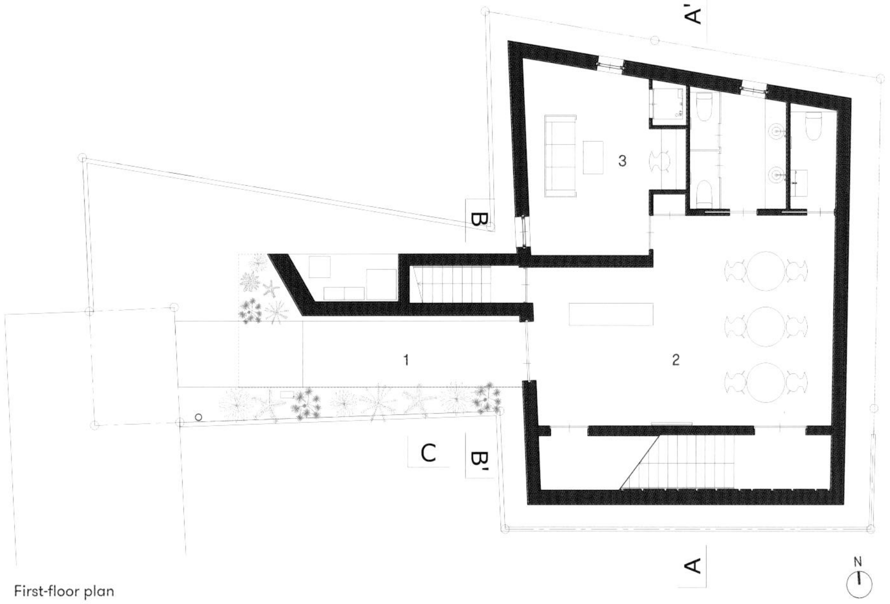

1. Approach
2. Entrance hall
3. Office
4. Backstage
5. Music salon
6. Corridor
7. Void
8. Storage

First-floor plan

Street view

1. Backstage
2. Approach
3. Storage
4. Music salon
5. Entrance hall

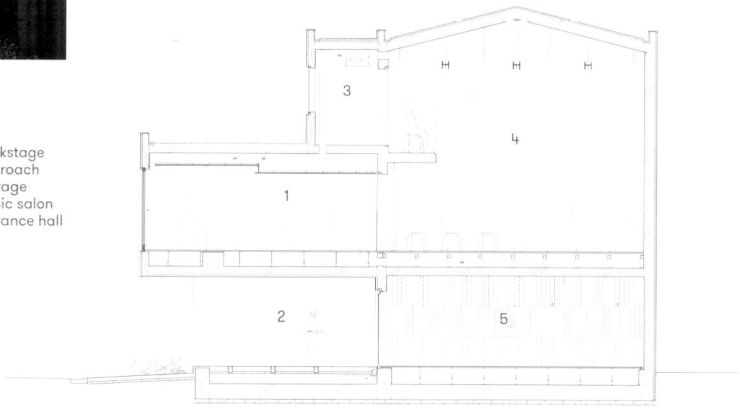

Detailed section

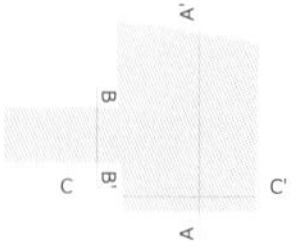

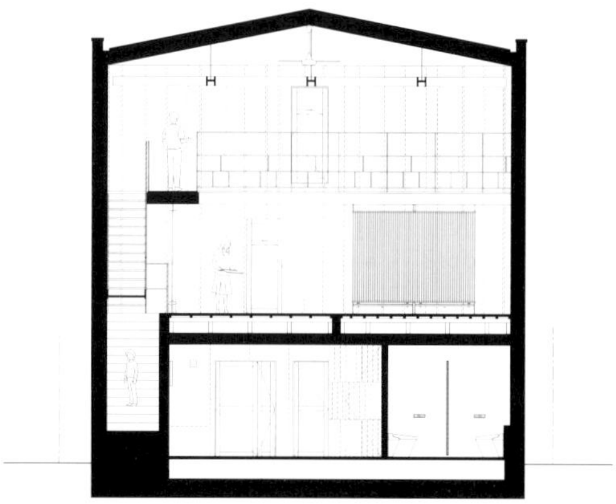

Section A-A'

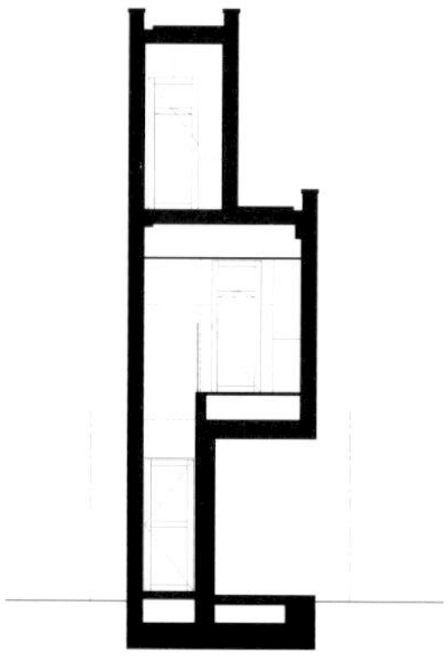

Section B-B'

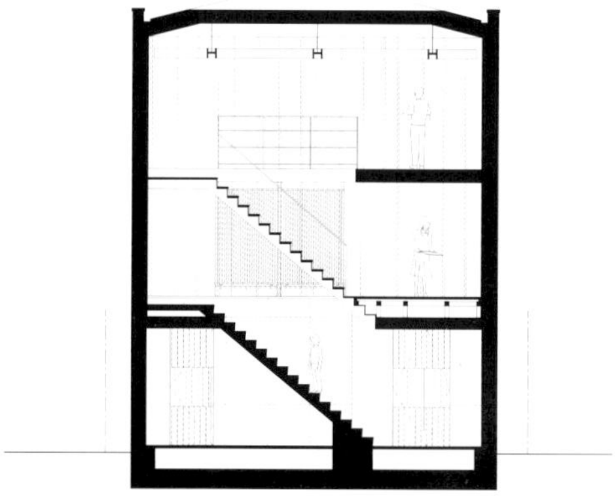

Section C-C'

Wanping Theater

Main entrance

Architect firm: Tongji Architectural Design (Group) Co., Ltd.
Principal architect: Xu Feng
Design team: Yin Peng, Zhou Jun, Ju Wei, Zhou You, Zeng Gang, Wang Heng, Liao Shulong
Location: Shanghai, China
Area: 29,281 square meters
Completion date: June 2021
Photography: Ma Yuan

The Wanping Theater project is located on the original site of Wanping Theater in Xuhui District, Shanghai. Committed to becoming the most influential opera performance space at home and abroad, it integrates the functions of a performance and exhibition center, cultural inheritance experience center, education promotion center, and cultural exchange center to form a professional opera platform. As an important public cultural facility at the municipal level, this project seeks to become a Shanghai urban cultural landmark. The project building includes 1,000 opera theaters, 300 small theaters, and several rehearsal halls, with a total construction area of 29,281 square meters, of which the aboveground construction area constitutes 15,853 square meters and the underground construction area constitutes 13,428 square meters. The building height is 23.95 meters and there are four floors located above ground level in the front area of the theater. In the rear, there are five floors aboveground and three floors underground.

Detail of façade

The architectural shape and spatial layout skillfully use Chinese elements to create an international architecture embellished with Shanghai-style cultural characteristics. The architectural shape is based on Shanghai-style jade carvings: the external volume is simple and thick, and the internal space is flexible and colorful; the façade is inspired by Chinese folding fans and features hanging glazed white ceramic plates, with straight lines and a continuous extension to form a gentle curved surface.

The inner performance space is projected and turned into a giant screen backdropped by the city, like a Chinese painting or the calligraphy strokes on a traditional Chinese fan. In terms of layout, it is inspired by the traditional courtyard, forming an introverted spatial pattern in the tensely distributed land. The interior space design samples traditional Chinese gardening techniques and displays a three-dimensional layout of large and small theaters and rehearsal spaces interspersed with opera education space. Overall, it shapes a complex space with stages and layers of performance areas everywhere, presenting a three-dimensional opera garden scene. At the same time, the core performance space is professionally and meticulously designed to meet the needs of a variety of theater performances and rehearsals.

Bird's-eye view

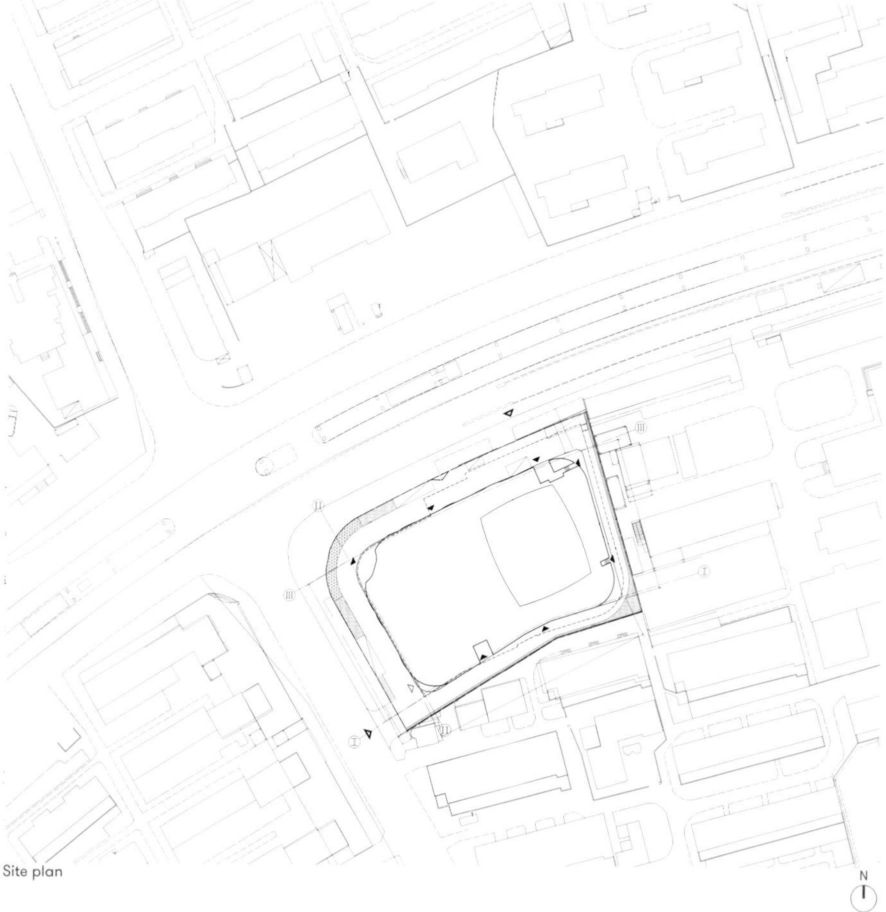

Site plan

West elevation

North elevation

Auditorium

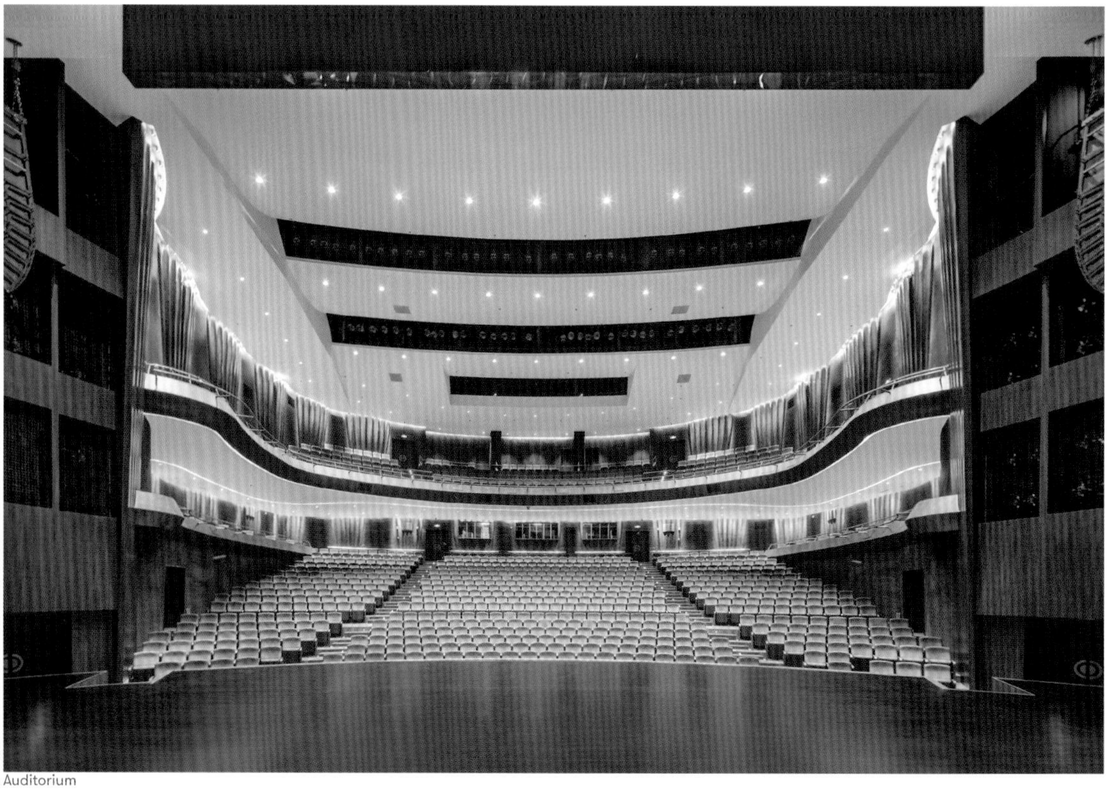
Auditorium

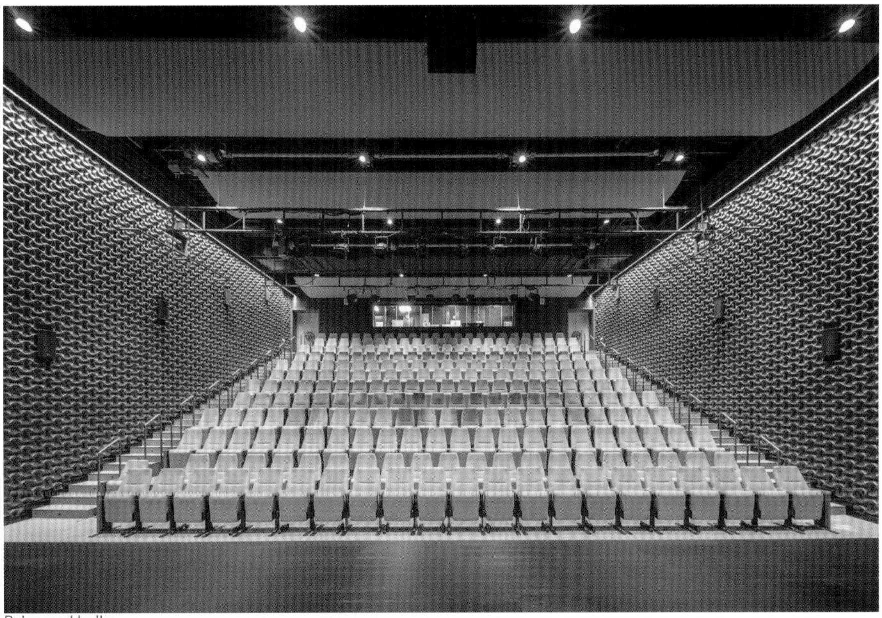
Rehearsal hall

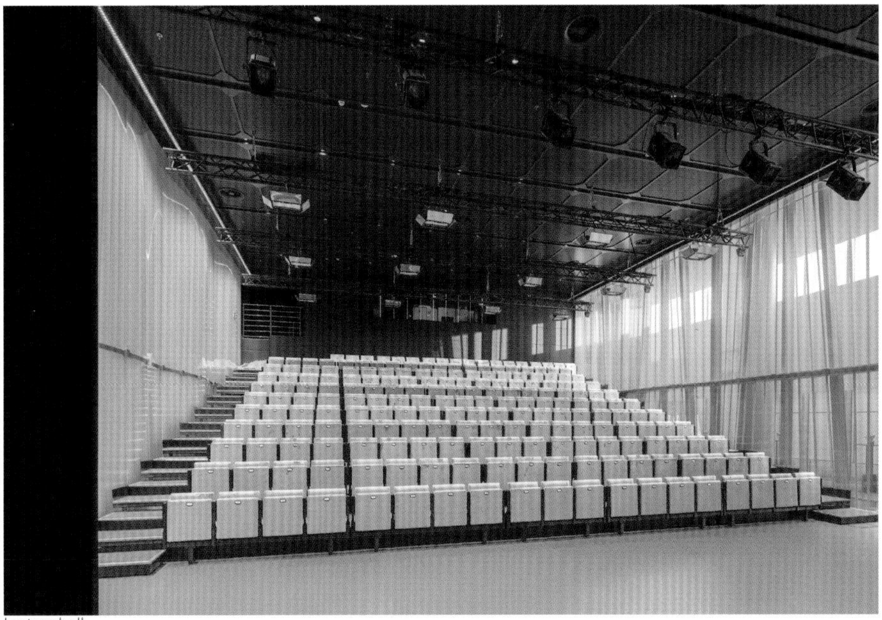
Lecture hall

Foyer

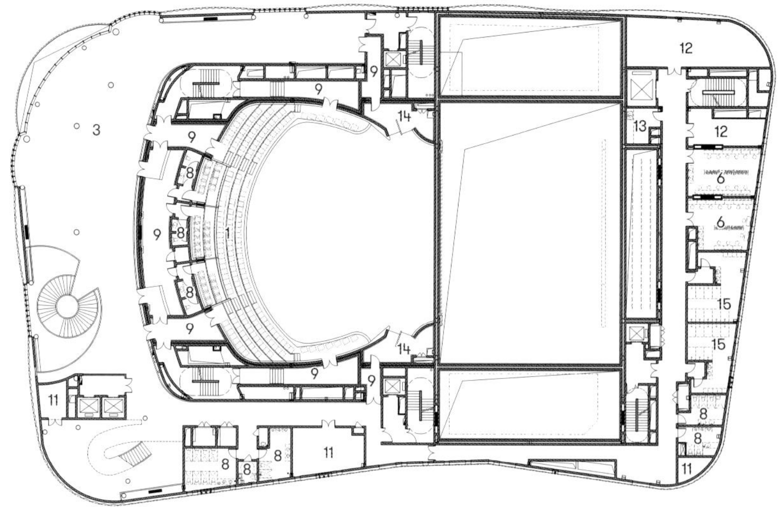

Third-floor plan

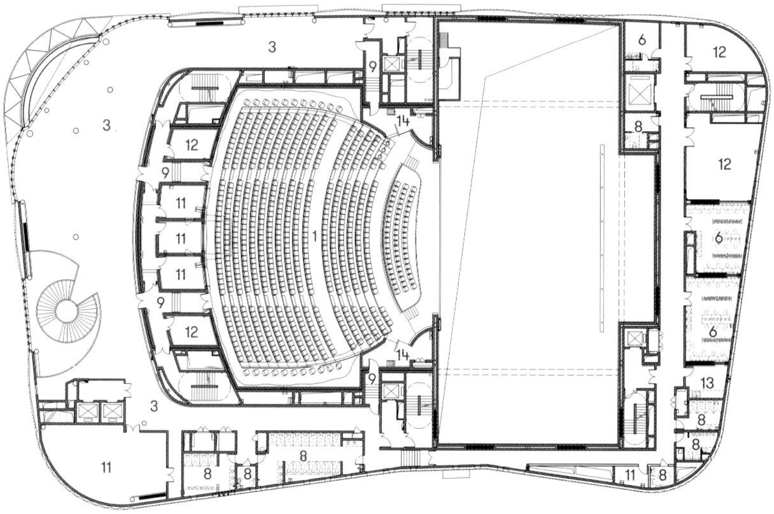

Second-floor plan

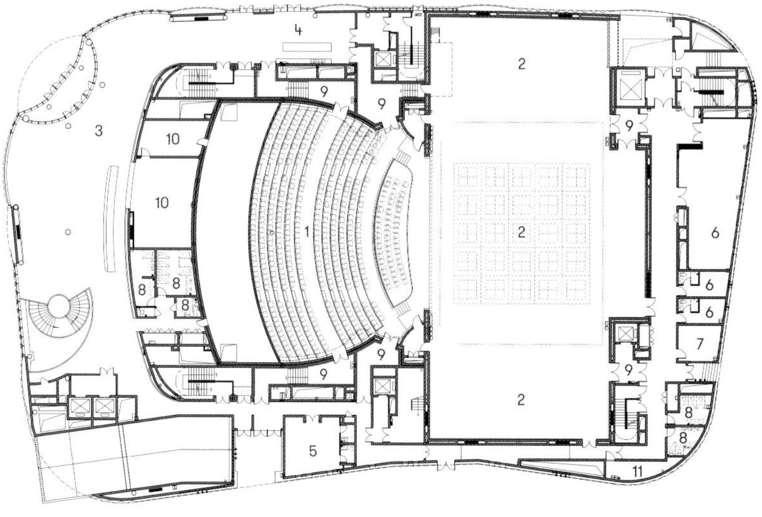

First-floor plan

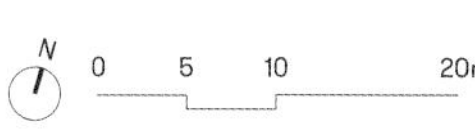

1. Auditorium
2. Stage
3. Foyer
4. Ticket office
5. VIP room
6. Powder room
7. Entrance
8. Toilet
9. Sound gates
10. Cloakroom
11. Electrical room
12. Office
13. Pantry
14. Side light room
15. Shower room

Main entrance: night view

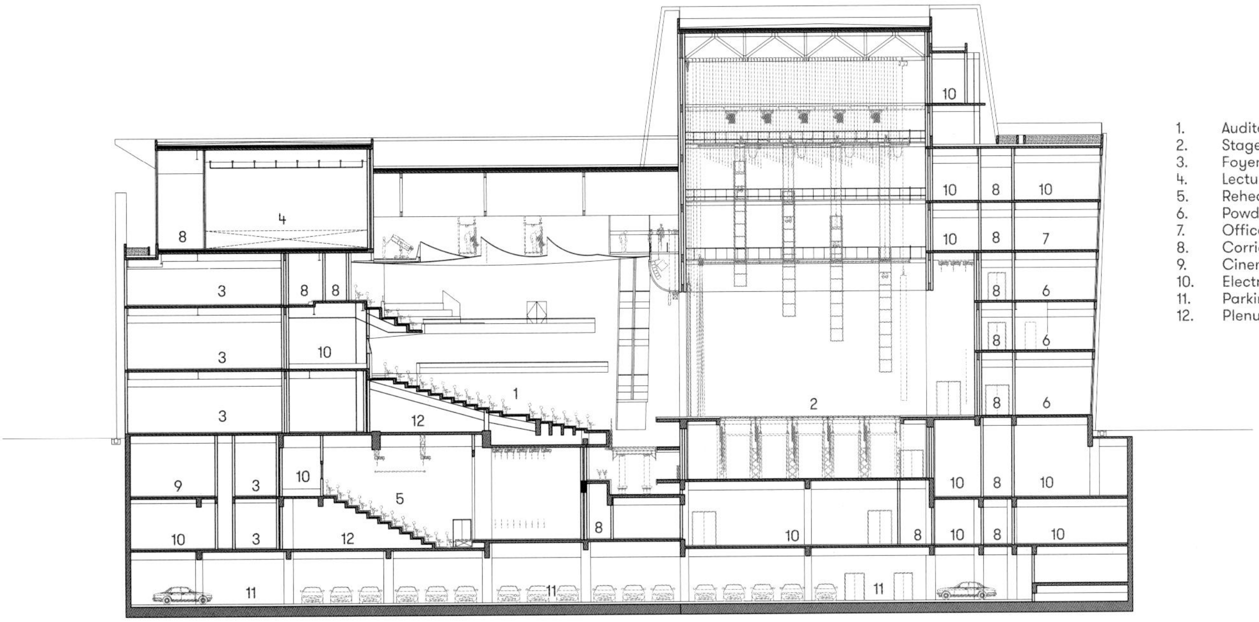

1. Auditorium
2. Stage
3. Foyer
4. Lecture hall
5. Rehearsal hall
6. Powder room
7. Office
8. Corridor
9. Cinema
10. Electrical room
11. Parking
12. Plenum

Section

0 5 10 20m

Athenia High School

View of overall school

Architect firm: Studio Next
Principal architect: Tarun Kumar
Design team: Tarun Kumar, Rajiv Gupta, ST.AR Structural Consultants
Client team: Amit Khurana, Jawahar Singh
Area: Phase 1—4,000 square meters (total 11,000 square meters)
Completion date: (Phase 1) December 2016
Photography: Aadit Basu

Athenia High school, built on a 13.5-acre site is located along Saharanpur-Dehradun highway, a main thoroughfare. The site previously housed a brick-baking kiln, which has since been abandoned, giving leeway to nature to tailor a sweep of serene, green, natural surroundings that provide a vibrant setting for an activity focused K-12 school (a school that is open to students from kindergarten to pre-university level).

The school advocates a transformative learning experience, where students grow both in and out of the classroom. The G+1 junior school building is primarily designed to trigger the senses. The built environment sensitizes the students to color, light, texture, smell, and sound. The students are always connected to the outdoors, having a constant view of outdoor spaces as they move through the building, enabling them to experience various sounds, smell, and the morphing natural daylight that changes through the day. A variety of natural materials add tactility and a color awareness to the experience through varied textures and colors in the form of exposed brick and concrete (on the façade), and mosaic and Kota stone flooring. Openings and brick *jaalis* (screens) allow the play of light on walls and surfaces at various locations, which change through the day as the sun moves. The outdoor spaces act as an extension of the classroom and promote participatory engagement; they seamlessly integrate with indoor spaces to resonate the school's "open" ideology.

Ample natural light, conducive cross ventilation, projections, and *jaalis* achieve a comfortable environment in the classrooms, while reducing energy consumption significantly. The school runs entirely on photovoltaics set on the rooftop. The use of natural materials, minimal plaster on the walls, and the optimum use of bricks and natural stone not only contribute to a low carbon footprint, but also reduce the overall maintenance cost of the building. This is also aided by construction techniques, such as in the boundary wall, which uses "rat-trap bond," a type of brick-laying technique that reduces the overall amount of brick used.

Athenia High School is not merely a building, but an attempt to create a legacy for a transformative learning environment, where the students are always ready to explore to reach greater heights.

View of entry landscape

View of school: a seamless inside-outside

View of courtyard: a seamless inside-outside

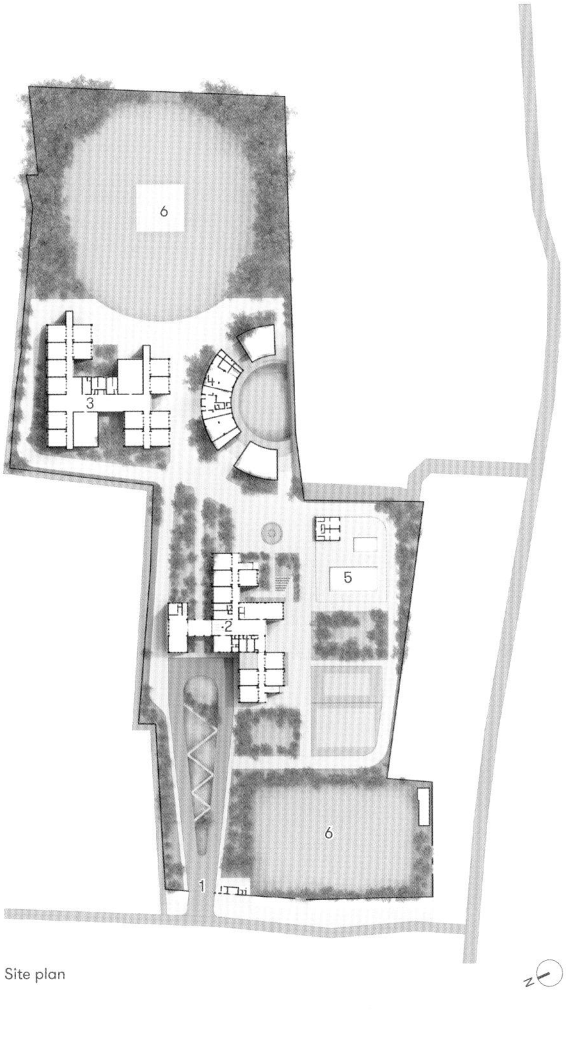

1. Entry
2. Junior block
3. Senior block
4. Common facilities
5. Swimming pool
6. Playground

Site plan

Central staircase

View of staircase

View of common space

Classroom

Science laboratory

Computer laboratory

View of corridor: light play in performance

1. Entrance lobby
2. Administration/library
3. Principal's office
4. Reception/waiting area
5. Medical room
6. Doctor's cabin
7. Classsroom
8. Science lab
9. Computer lab
10. Storage/server
11. Faculty room

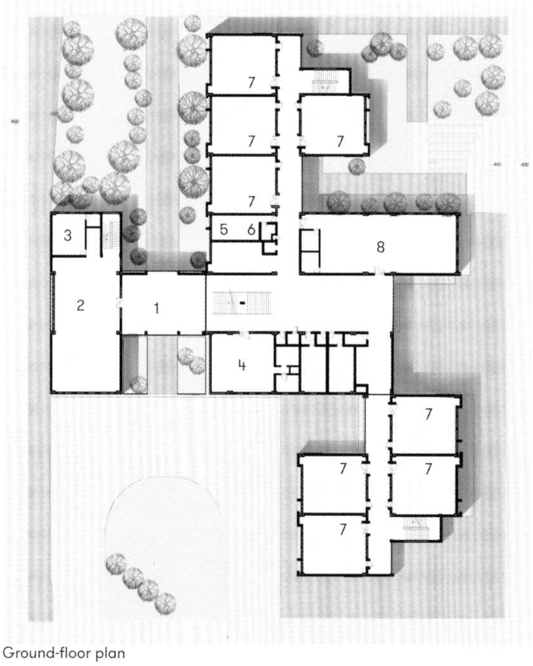

Ground-floor plan

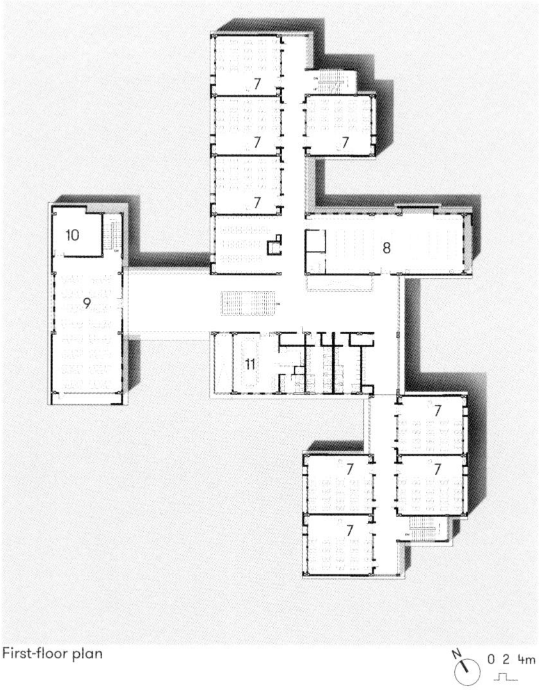

First-floor plan

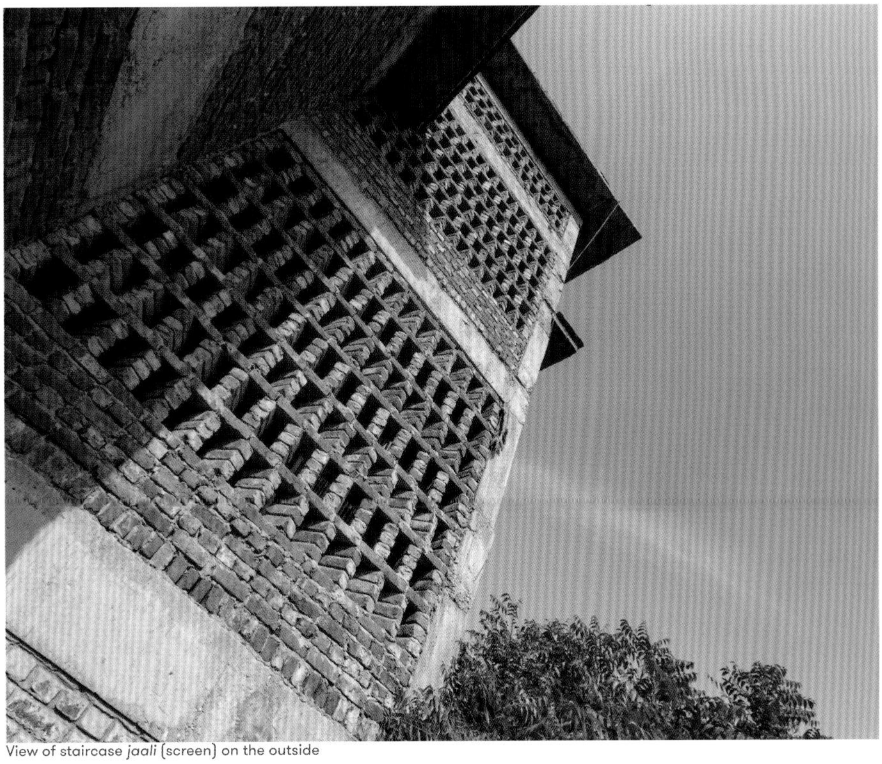
View of staircase *jaali* (screen) on the outside

View of building in landscape

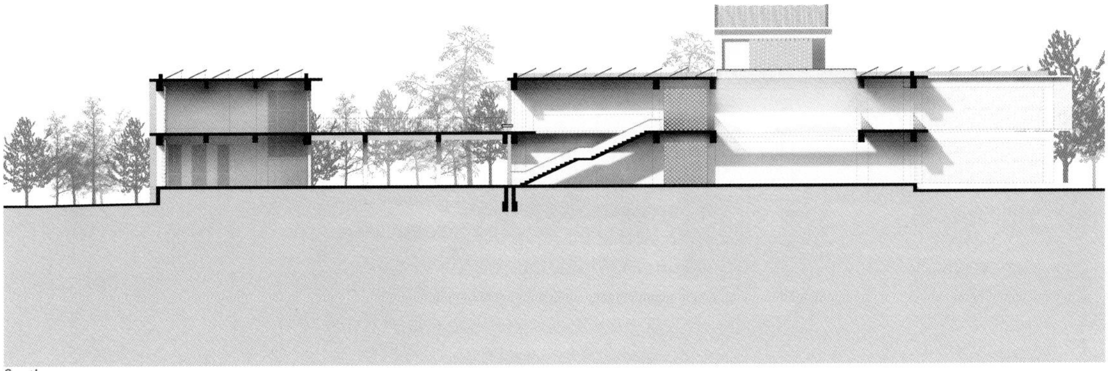
Section

Rane Vidyalaya

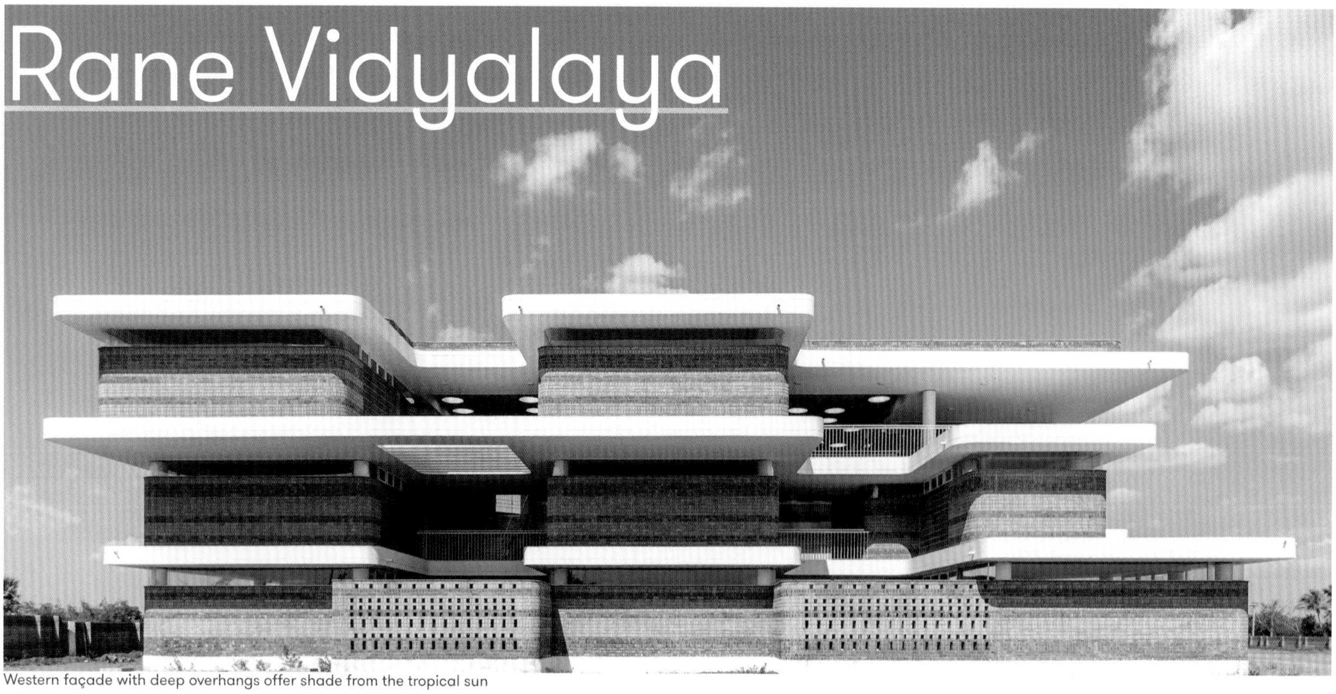

Western façade with deep overhangs offer shade from the tropical sun

Architect firm: Shanmugam Associates
Principal architect: Shanmugam A, Raja Krishnan D, Santhosh Shanmugam
Design team: Srinivasan, Satish Kumar, Balasubramaniam, Mohammed Ismail, Rukmani Thangam, Praveen Kumar
Location: Trichy, India
Area: 50,000 square feet
Completion date: 2018
Photography: LINK Studio, Bangalore

Rane Vidyalaya CBSE school, a CSR initiative by Rane Foundation India Pvt. Ltd., a leading industrial conglomerate, is a K-12 campus that takes in students from the kindergarten level to the 12th grade.

Theerampalayam, the rural region where the school is located, has no proper educational institutions that offer quality learning. The closest city, Tiruchirapalli, which is a Tier-II city in the state of Tamil Nadu, India is 20 kilometers away. The neighborhood districts are a mix of small, rural villages, where the main occupation is agriculture and unskilled labor.

The project was executed in two phases. Presently Phase 1 has been constructed, with an area of 50,000 square feet (4,645 square meters). The intent was to create an infrastructure that would have a positive social impact on the local community and also showcase the core values of Rane.

Regional construction techniques, a structured pedagogy of the Indian educational system, and a construction cost of US$20 per square foot formed the basis of the design development. Inspiration was drawn from the sixth-century-built Thiruvellarai temple's walls and the layered cross sections of fifty-year-old houses in the region. Following the consistent construction methodology revealed in these structures, a layering starting from huge random rubble and stone at the bottom, to finer solid brick work, mud, and slate on top was adopted in the walls. Alternating layers of red wire cut bricks—from the local kiln—and gray fly ash brick—recycled from industrial cement waste—were used.

Kindergarten classrooms are designed to have individual gardens that encourage a seamless integration of the outdoor and indoor space. With every level-up in the school's class grade, the lessons become more functional, so as to introduce structured learning. To facilitate this, the overall design approach avoids sharp edges in the walls, columns, slab edges, and in every detail possible, to ensure the safety of students.

As the site is located on the tropical belt of interior Tamil Nadu, the design makes use of natural ventilation in the space, along with natural lighting. All walls are stopped at lintel height and have openable windows above to allow hot air to dissipate and to increase cross ventilation. Terra cotta *jaalis* (screens) are also used as secondary shading devices. Incorporating significant openings along the predominant southeast–northwest wind direction and minor wind tunnels in the east-west direction between classrooms creates a comfortable microclimate in the building.

Taking inspiration from temple mandapams, where huge gatherings take place, an enclosed central courtyard with perforated lightwells in the roof is planned. This courtyard, placed so that it is visually connected at all levels, serves as a multifunctional place of congregation for lunch breaks, school assembly, exhibitions, co-curricular training, and small gatherings.

The architectural features incorporated in the building—such as the red solid bricks, baked earth tiles, terra cotta *jaali*, and gray fly ash bricks—help address the micro climate in the space, facilitate ventilation, create interesting light and shade experiences through roof perforations, and provide safe, green courtyards where the children can enjoy the outdoors. At the same time, they also articulate the design language of the local region, while creating a fun, educational environment. Through sourcing materials from surrounding locations, a wholesome cost-effective architectural solution is deployed.

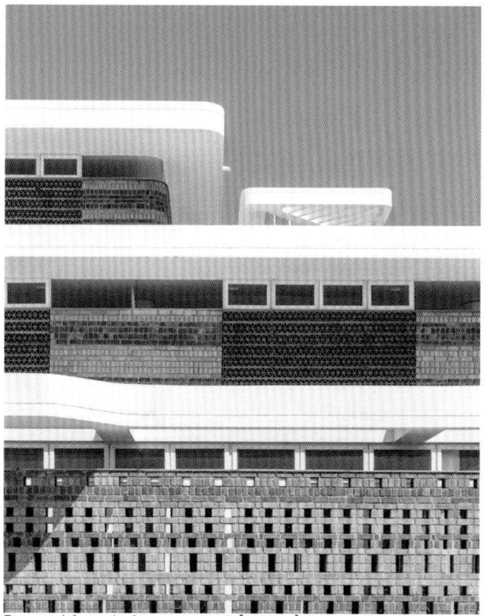

External façade features *jaali* (screen) openings and 7-foot-high walls to create fenestration and natural cooling within the classrooms

1. Main entry
2. Security room
3. Phase 1
4. Phase 2
5. Basketball court
6. Volleyball court
7. Badminton court
8. Football field and running track
9. Service entry

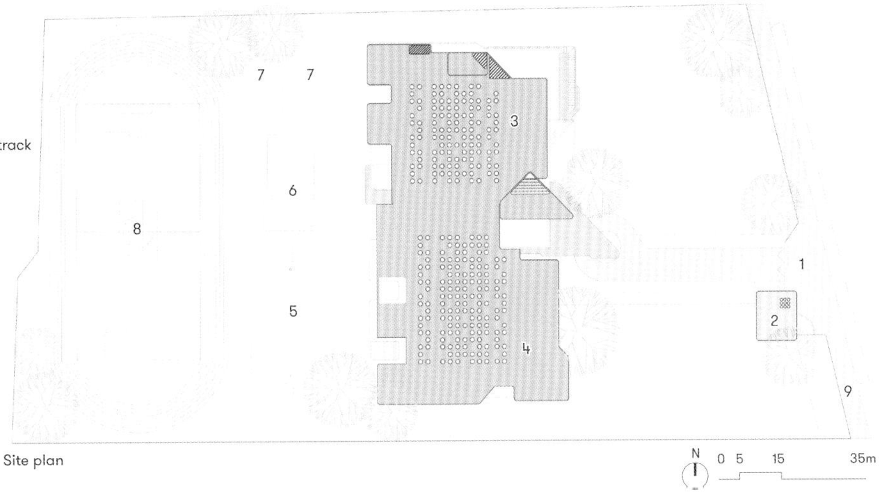

Site plan

The unplastered walls on the western façade are a pattern themselves

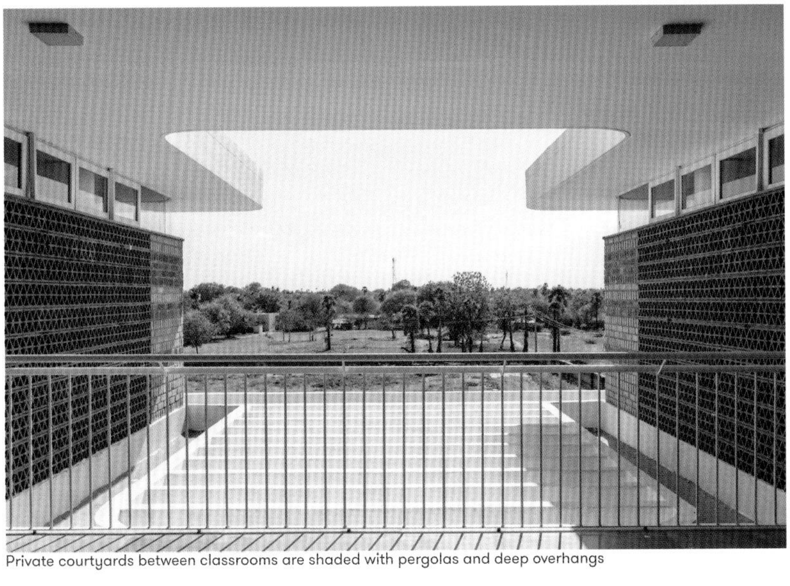
Private courtyards between classrooms are shaded with pergolas and deep overhangs

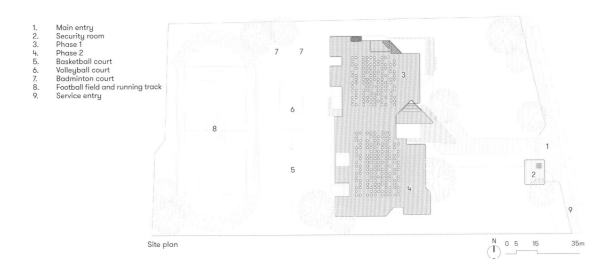

Main entry with drop-off zone from the eastern side

A unique façade pattern was designed on-site with the contractor using locally sourced fly ash bricks, wire cut bricks, and terra cotta *jaali*

Abundant natural lighting and corridors overlooking each other were created across the various floors, thereby creating a vertical interactive connection of spaces

The internal multipurpose courtyard acts as the central point of congregation

The central courtyard roof has circular openings finished with glass covers, allowing the light to form patterns on the floor below

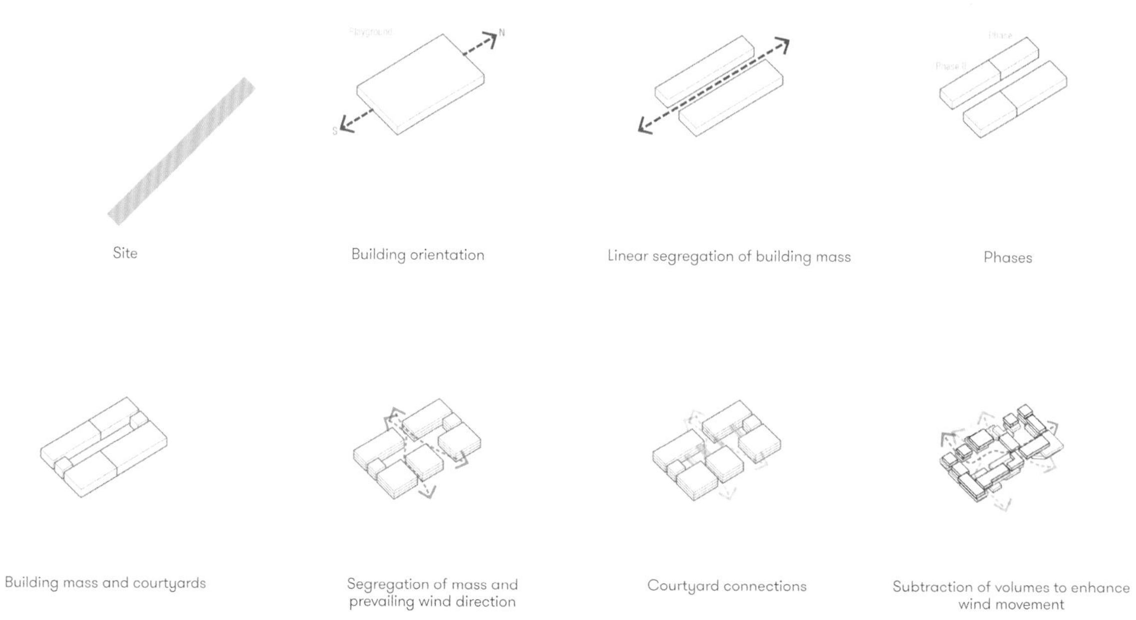

Design development

A lean budget stipulated that materials be used effectively and cost be minimized without compromising design

Connecting bridges create interesting volumes for the children to explore

Kindergarten classrooms are visually connected, facilitating ease of monitoring the children, ensuring their safety at all times

Classrooms on the ground floor are planned with their own private courtyards for free play and spill-over activities like "show-and-tell" and storytelling sessions

Second-floor plan

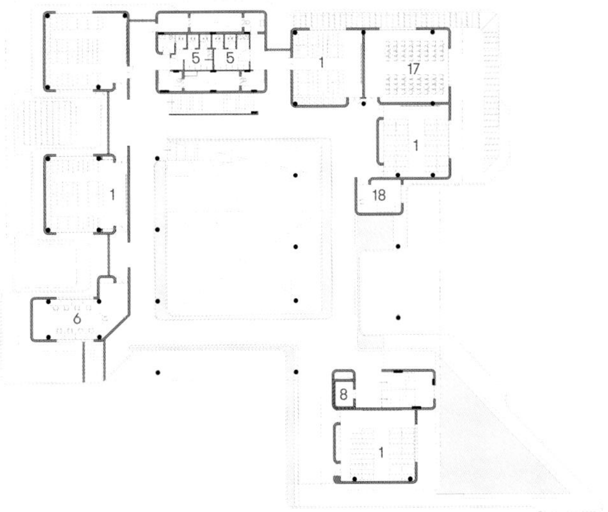

First-floor plan

1. Classroom
2. Outdoor play area
3. Multipurpose room
4. Library
5. Restrooms
6 Staff room
7. Board room
8. Elevator
9. Administration room
10. Waiting room
11. Vice-principal's office
12. Principal's office
13. Storage room
14. Assembly
15. Portico
16. Electrical room
17. Audio-visual room
18. Sick room

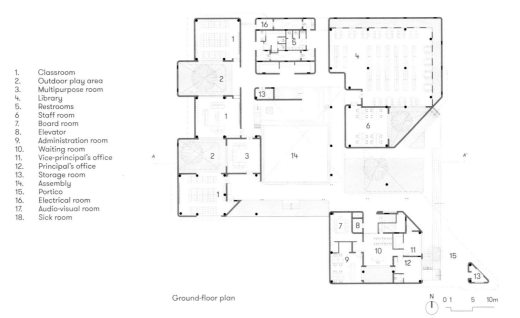

Ground-floor plan

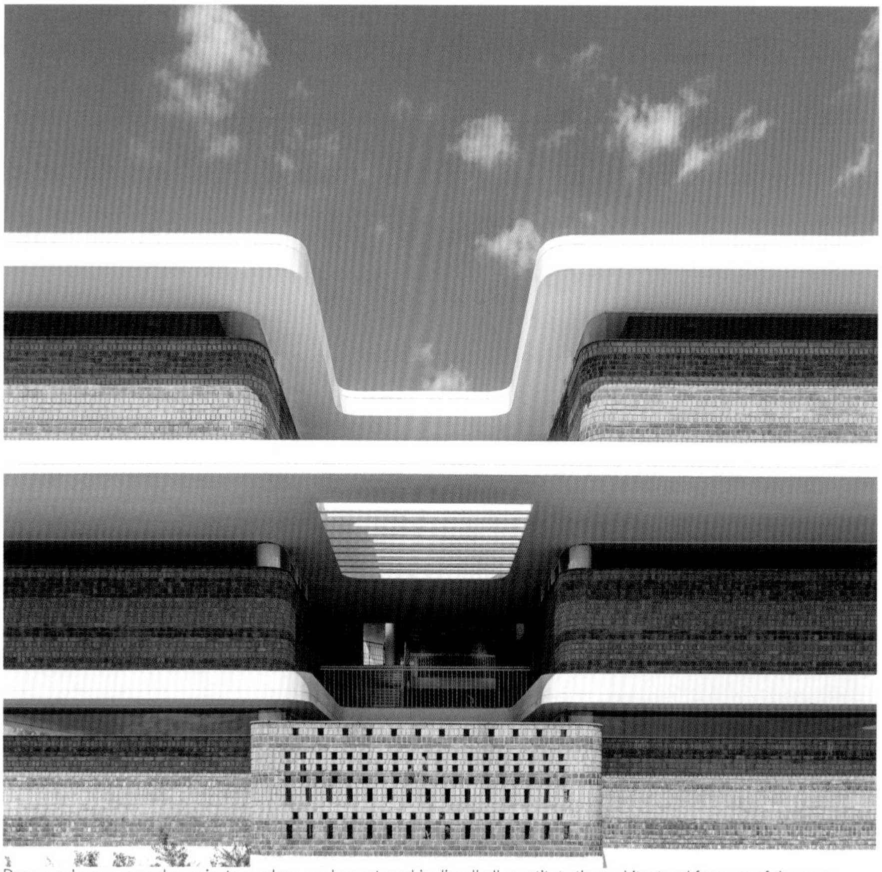

Deep overhangs, pergolas, private gardens, and an external *jaali* wall all constitute the architectural features of the open spaces of Rane Vidyalaya school

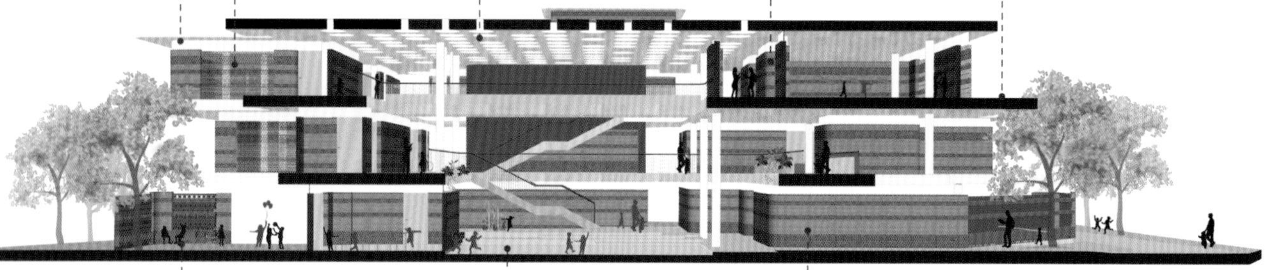

Walls end 8 inches below the roof. Openable glass windows are installed above the walls to facilitate cross ventilation inside classrooms. The glass windows also maximize daylight inside the classrooms.
Circular perforations on the roof fill the volume below with ample natural light, allowing the courtyard to be used for assembly and other gatherings. The perforations cast shadows on the planes below that shift throughout the day, creating an interesting shadow play.
Deep roof overhangs offer shade from the sun.
Terra cotta *jaali* walls are used as a secondary skin, aiding in heat reduction, while offering maximum safety for children.
All edges and structural members in the building are rounded, further ensuring the safety of children.
The garden play area strategically placed between two classrooms encourages interaction. This enclosed, shaded play area creates a comfortable microclimate within, allowing children to utilize the space with minimum supervision during the day. The garden play areas are also used as outdoor classrooms and are visually connected to the indoors.
The triple-height central courtyard opens up the volume and is visually connected at all levels. The courtyard is used for assembly and other activities like indoor games, meetings, and also as a lunch/dining space for children.
Walls are constructed with layers of red brick and recycled fly ash brick procured from the local kiln. This layering is inspired from regional construction methodologies.

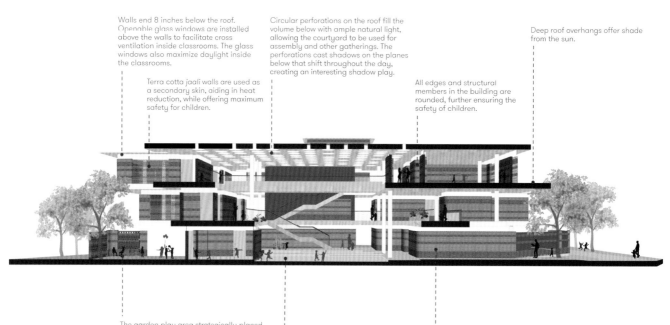

Section AA'

Suzhou Urban Planning Exhibition Hall

On-site photo of the east façade

Architect firm: Shenzhen AUBE Architectural Engineering Design Consultants Co., Ltd.
Principal architect: Mao Dong, Ding Rong, Wang Shi, Zhou Yi
Design team: Wu Zhiyang, Tan Bochao, Zhou Xingyu, Liu Minjuan, Lei Tianfeng, Cai Hui
Location: Suzhou, China
Area: 29,789.19 square meters
Completion date: May 2018
Photography: Tian Fangfang

With its architectural space being open and inclusive, Suzhou Urban Planning Exhibition Hall aims to actively welcome civic life as a part of it by organizing rich, entertaining activities for the public. The design scheme dug deeply into the local context and its uniqueness, and forms a spatial organization that naturally makes the architecture a regional cultural landmark of the area. The square-shaped building sits on one side of the site, covering the major functions of display space and office. Inspired by the Lingbi stone, the building abstractly portrays, with contemporary techniques, a cultural landmark that is solid but airy, simple yet versatile, and constantly changing, in the process creating a variety of public spaces that offer multiple possibilities of use for the citizens.

The main entrance is set on the ground floor; the grand steps on the side of the building can also guide the pedestrian flow up from the square to the secondary entrance on the first floor. The "vein cut" concept cantilevers a part of the first floor, providing a covered venue for public events, while the "cross-cut" approach divides the building volume above its base, establishing an integral architectural image while keeping the separate functions of exhibition hall and office relatively independent. The office part is placed on the north side, echoing the administrative center to the north of Suzhou Urban Planning Exhibition Hall. The cuts, both horizontal and vertical, help reduce the sense of oppression evoked by the monolithic volume of the building, reflecting "thin."

In order to further create more public spaces of diversity and fun, a number of atriums, side courtyards, terraces, and gardens are scattered throughout the building. Bridges, partitions, and glass screens also facilitate the movement between interior and exterior spaces, forming a pleasant relationship between the solid and the void. The exhibition spaces are interspersed with courtyards to compose a series of indoor spaces with rhythmic variations; meanwhile, the spatial hierarchy gets enriched and all functional units are interconnected vertically, representing "airy."

The design takes advantage of "narrow lanes" and "courtyards" to form a "hollow structure with multiple wind tunnels." The "narrow lanes" conform to the dominant wind directions of summertime, encouraging the natural winds to enter at a low level and exit high, which—in combination with the updraft of heated air—strengthens natural ventilation; in the winter, plants in the courtyard block prevailing winds and improve indoor comfort, representing "porous."

The façade design derives from the creased appearance of the Lingbi stone. Simplified and abstracted, a pattern composed of the positive and the negative is formed and reinterpreted with glassfiber-reinforced-concrete (GRC); and with reliefs on solid walls that do not require natural lighting, the façades celebrate the play of light and shadow, reflecting "creased."

Suzhou Urban Planning Exhibition Hall not only performs as an exhibition space, but also provides the city with an open, vibrant, and experiential public space, fully exploring its nature as a cultural landmark, to attract citizens to visit and enjoy the space. The multilayered architectural space, integrated with cutting-edge display technology, is set to bolster the visitor experience, and overall, also enhance the "display" effect of the venue. The Suzhou Urban Planning Exhibition Hall will soon become the brand-new business card of Suzhou New District, activating its surrounding areas and improving the city's image.

Aerial view

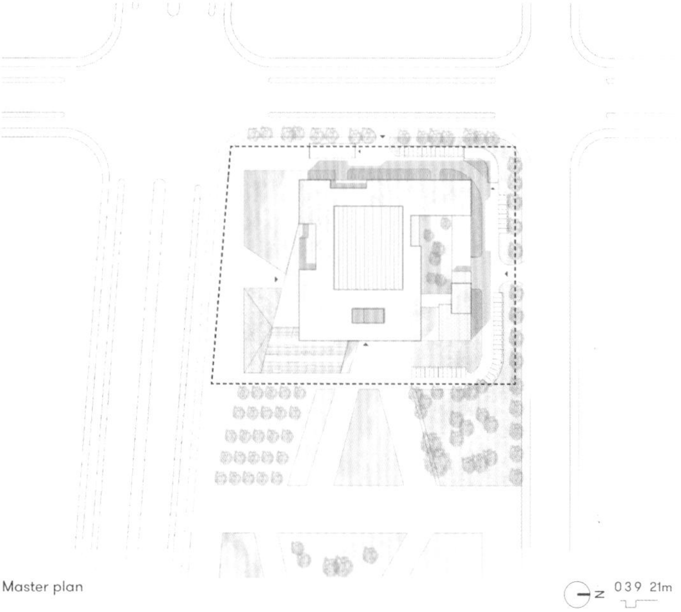
Master plan

Façade and terrace details

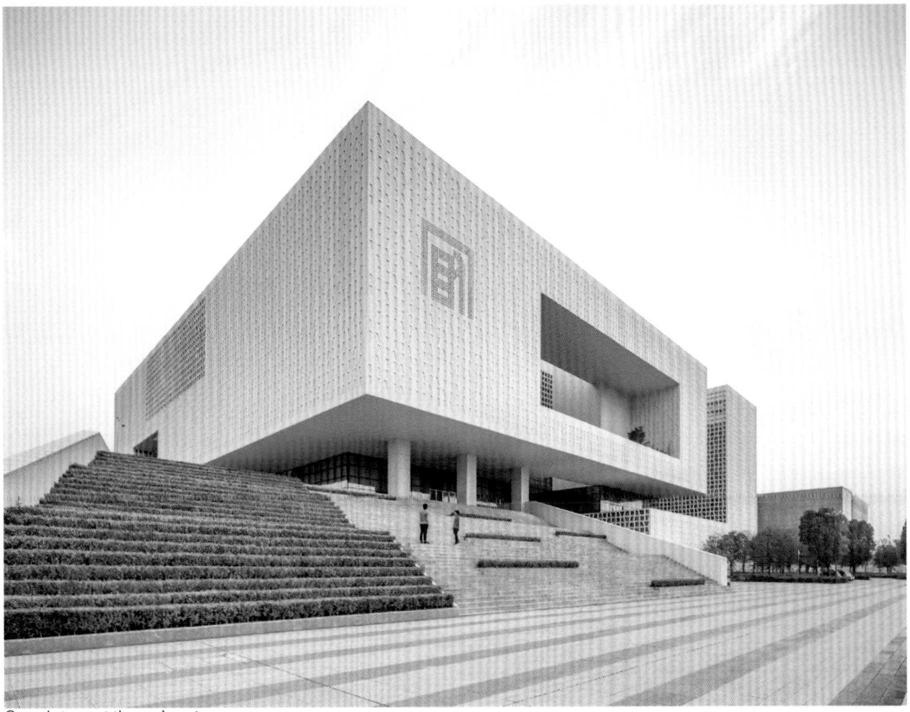
Grand steps at the main entrance

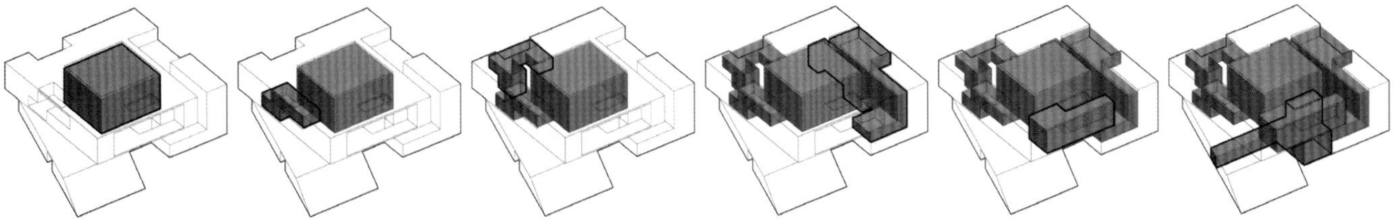
Diagram of solid-void spaces

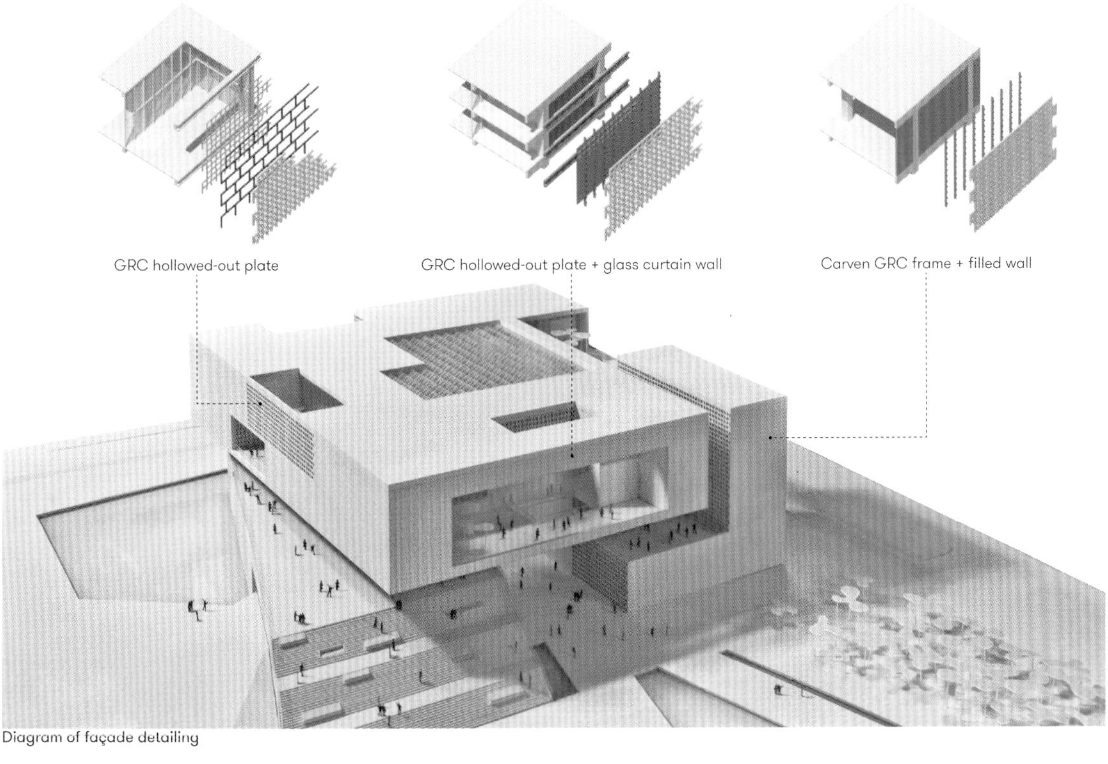

Diagram of façade detailing

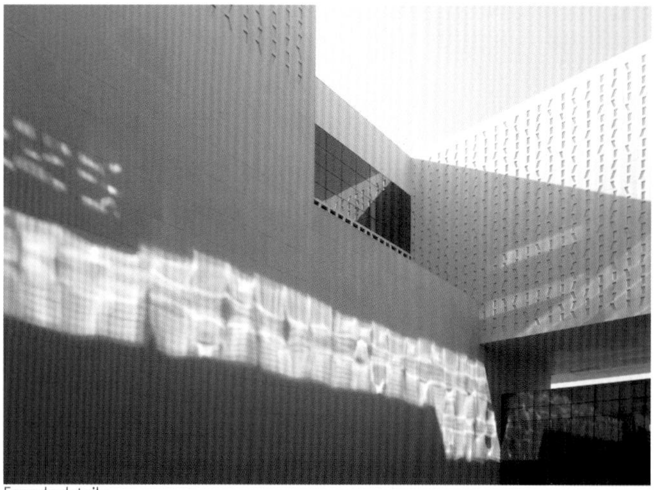
Façade details

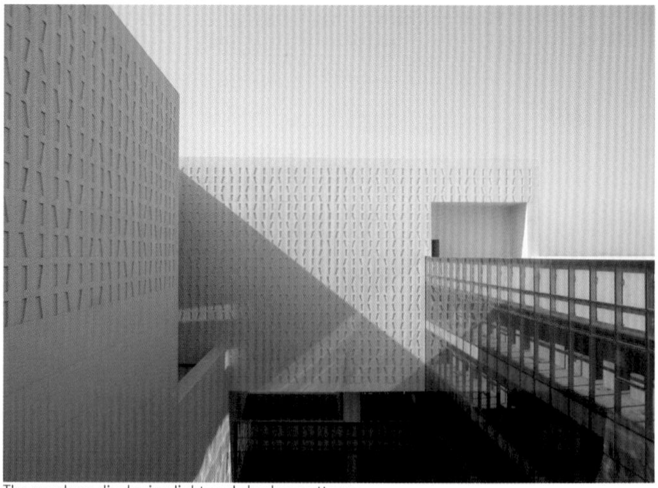
The envelope displaying light and shadow patterns

Hollow structure with multiple wind tunnels

Courtyard space

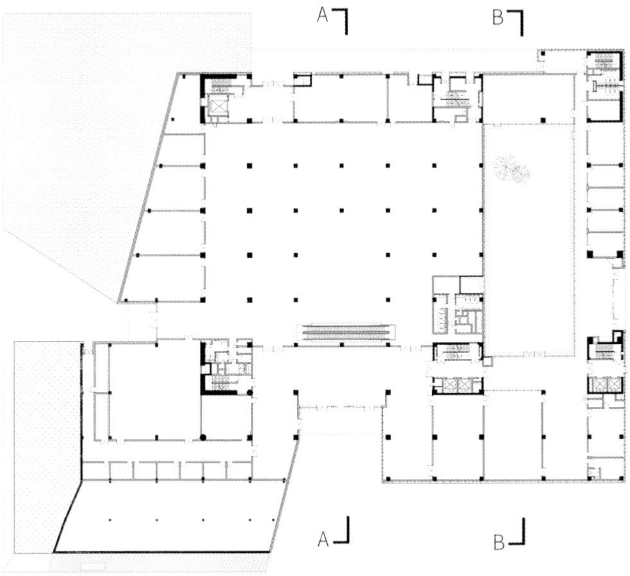

First-floor plan

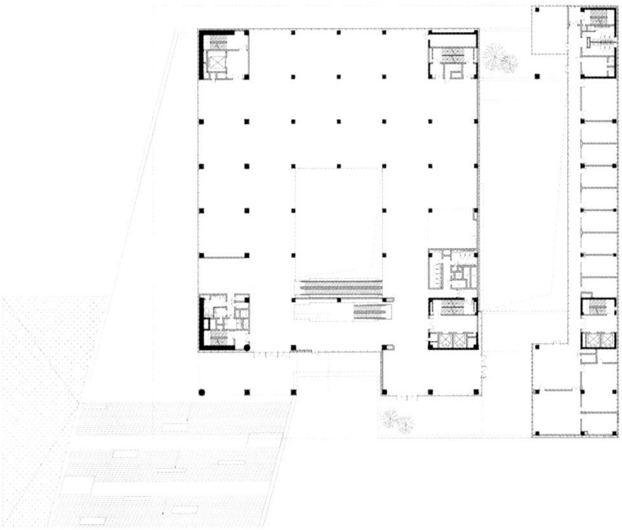
Second-floor plan

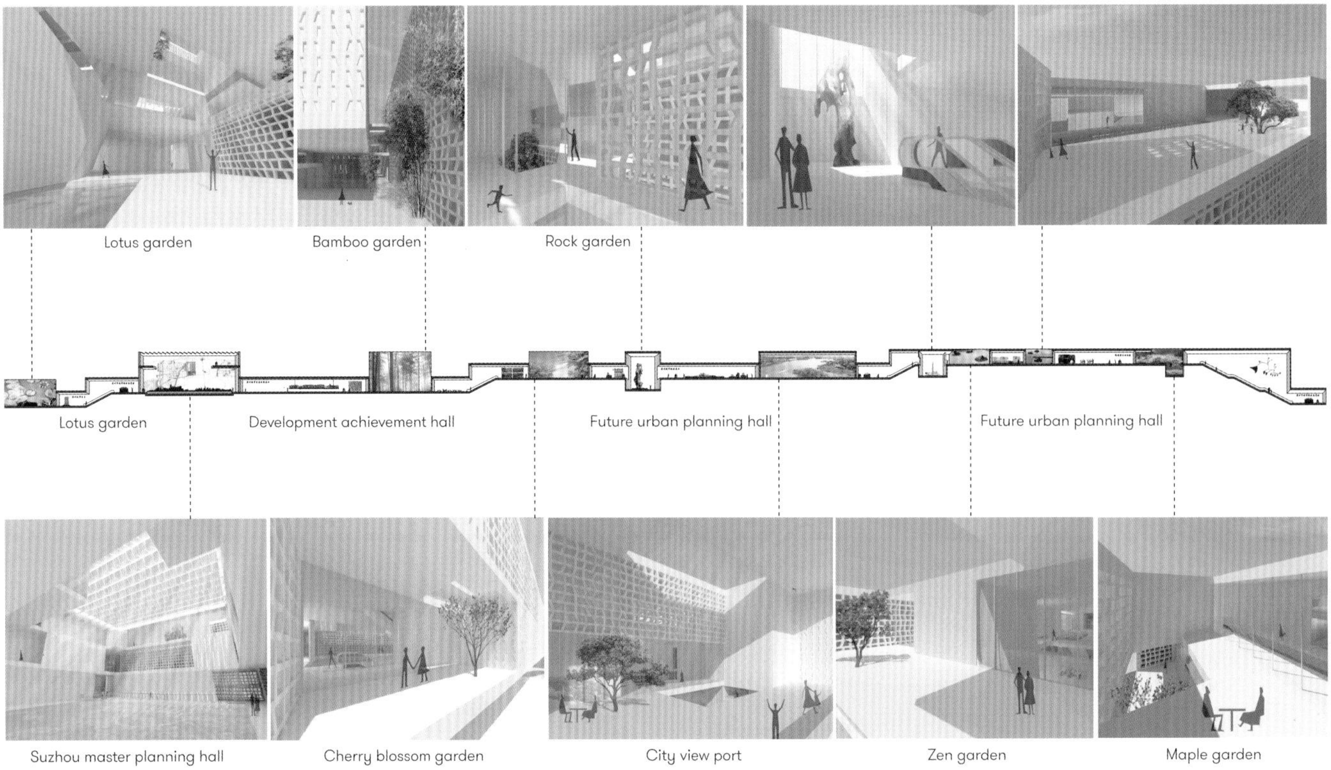

Continuous profile showing the journey within the buliding

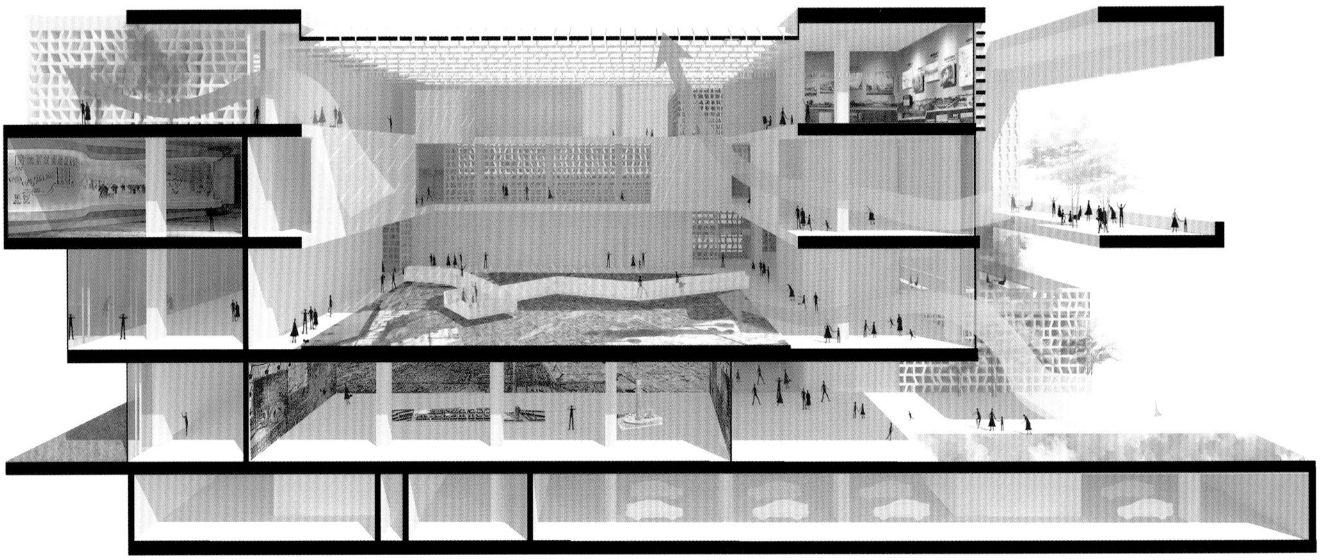

Diagram of permeable indoor-outdoor spaces and ventilation

South façade

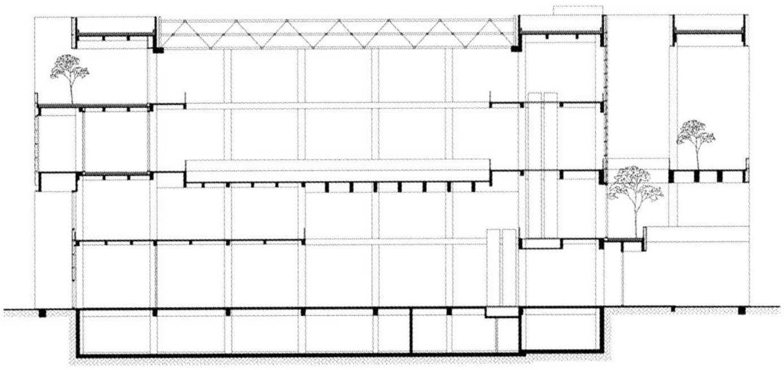
Section A-A

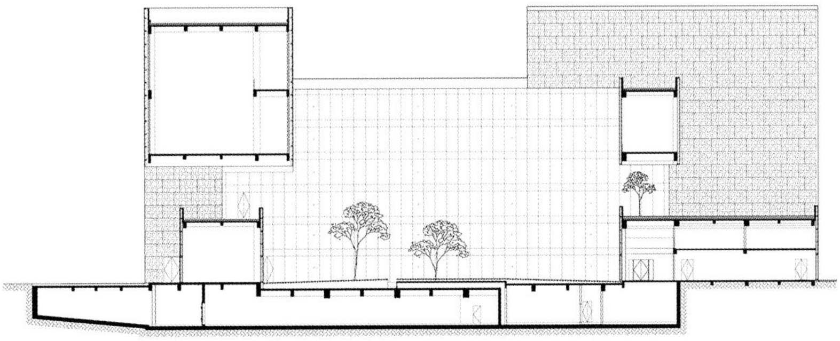
Section B-B

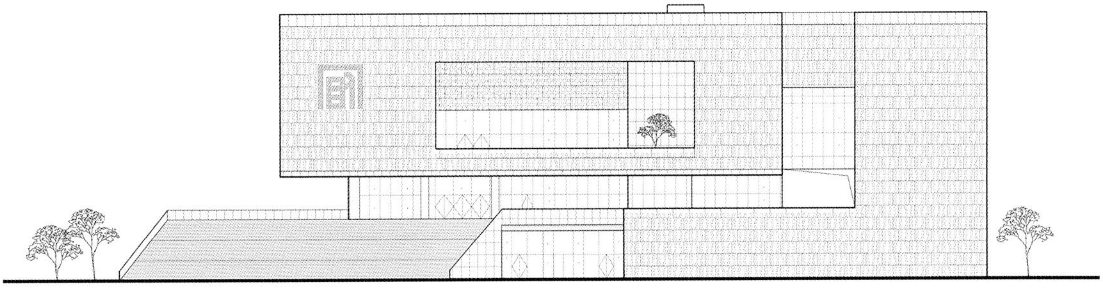
East elevation

Zhongguancun Digital Economy Innovation Industry Base

Atrium garden

Architect firm: QUCESS Design
Principal architect: Li Yiming
Design team: Li Jianchuan, Wang Lei, Wang Xueli, Zhao Zhiwei, Mu Yu, Zhang Zhihao
Location: Beijing, China
Area: 21,565 square meters
Completion date: May 2020
Photography: Zheng Yan

Located in the core of Zhongguancun, Xueqing Road Station is within 2 kilometers of Tsinghua University and Peking University. Most of the old factories in the area that remained from the industrial era were demolished and renewed, and the area has since become an unofficial hub for dot-com companies. The Beijing Research Institute of Mechanical and Electrical Technology (BRIMET) is one of the few survivors. Some thought was required in this renovation project to appropriately endow the building to effectively meet the needs of emerging internet and science-and-technology enterprises. A maximized working area with good ventilation, a properly lit environment, and a high-quality active atmosphere were among the main considerations in this project.

Although the project scope was mainly the interior renovation, the design team focused on the surroundings as well. In consideration of the location of the building entrance, the entire factory building was divided into four parts in a circular shape to integrate it into the environment outside. Under the challenges of a limited budget, an extensive structure, and high-tech requirements, it was crucial to question how the existing conditions could be used to maximize the office area and ensure that the building maintains a well-ventilated environment that features conducive interior lighting and an appealing atmosphere.

Together with the surrounding environment, the roof and the structural space below the original ground of the factory were also reconstructed. The height of this space and roof were also utilized to their optimal value.

The design concept surrounds every office area with a garden, so that staff can enjoy a moment of relaxation when they look out the window. The garden is also accessible to staff for short breaks to enjoy some sun and nature.

A large area of the original skylight has been expanded and transformed to guide the circulation according to the flow of light that permeates the building. The skylight connects to the atrium, so that the atrium garden is saturated in natural light. Come evening, as the sun slowly fades and night coyly makes it entrance, the skylight offers scenes of the dusky sky filled with the first

Building exterior after renovation

Stairs descending to the semi-underground space

appearance of glittering stars. Part of the skylight of the old building was retained in the second half of the atrium so that users could experience the unique traces of the original factory building within the space.

To balance the long east–west scale of the project, two spiral staircases of different shapes have been designed in the atrium to disperse and organize the flow of people, thereby playing a role in "activating" the atmosphere of the space. A glass brick façade at the far end of the atrium creates an illuminated "cove" that entices visitors to linger and enjoy the light and airy gallery-like ambiance, complete with transparent hemisphere swing seats.

Near one of the spiral stairs, two glass elevators echo the contemporary, breezy design language of the stairs; the structural steel frame of the elevators is painted with bright colors to form the visual anchor in the atrium. The artistic twists of the spiral staircase, contrasted against the industrialized elevator columns, add a feel of vitality to the space, lifting the ambiance, while imparting a quirkiness to the action of ascending and descending the stairs.

At the lowest level of the building, the original ground was dug to the foundation of the pillars to create a semi-underground garage to meet the demand for parking. The sunken atrium garden extends into this garage to add a dash of greenery to the usually somber concrete confines of a parking garage, as well as to tweak the stereotypical experience of a garage.

In the reconstruction of this old factory building, ensuring the safety of the building and structure was important, as too was how to make the most of the existing building and structural conditions, so as to keep construction costs low. To maximize the utilization rate, the roof supports almost all the electro-mechanical equipment of the building. Playing off that, two roof gardens, with different styles and functions for relaxing and gathering, are designed on the inclined roof of the original building and feature solar self-luminous seats and art installations. Accessible to the public during the day, as well as at night, these gardens also provide a respite from long work hours to employees who work in this and nearby buildings, so that they can gaze upon a starry sky as they allow the mind time to rest and wander.

New and old materials merge with each other in the space

Atrium garden

The spiral staircase in the space

The sunken atrium garden rewrites the typical parking garage formula, adding color and greenery to an otherwise somber gray space

The spiral staircase lifts the dimension of the space with creative quirkiness

The see-through transparent elevator echoes the creative flair of the spiral stairs

The elevator entrance on the fourth floor

The brightly painted structural steel frame of the elevator brightens the space

The bright yellow of the elevators' structural frame forms a visual anchor and draws the eye

The spiral staircase snakes its way up in elegant curves

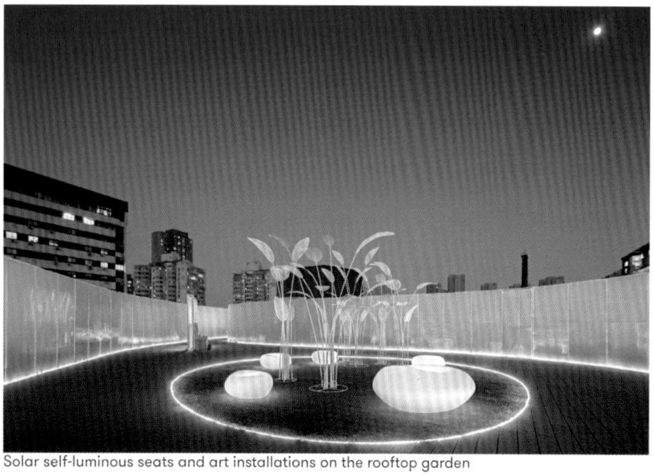

Solar self-luminous seats and art installations on the rooftop garden

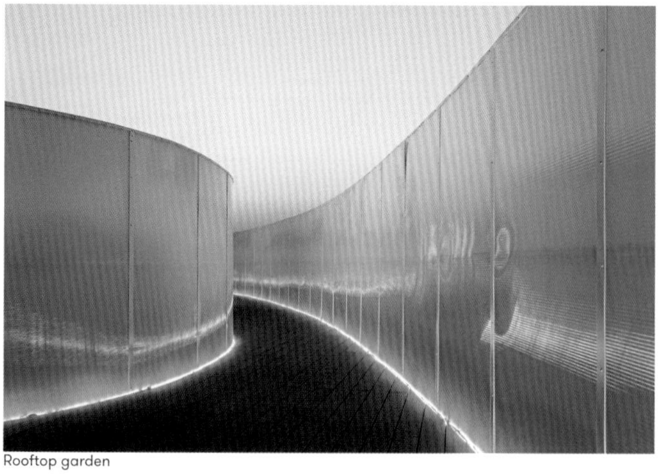

Rooftop garden

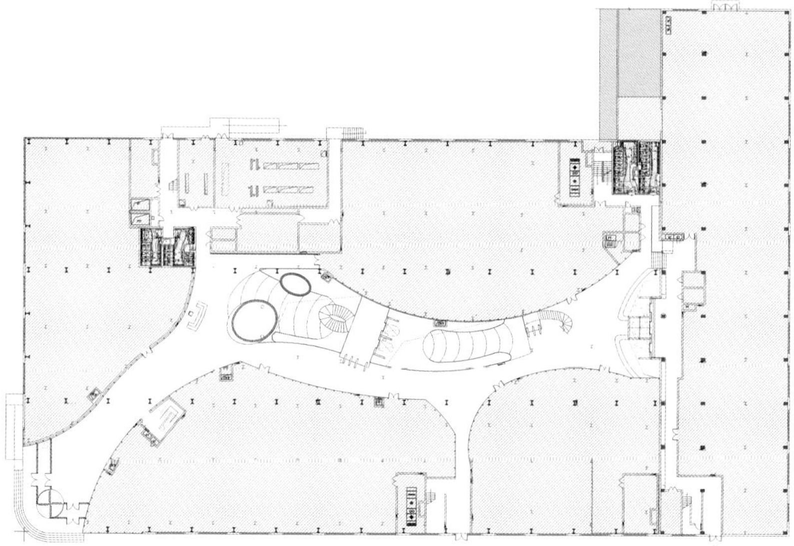

First-floor plan

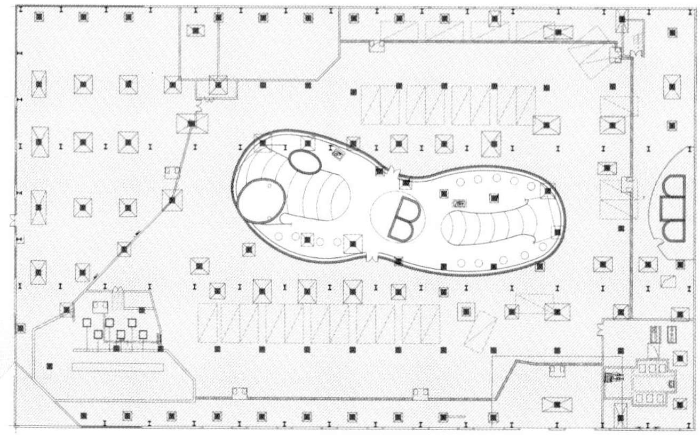

Underground-floor plan

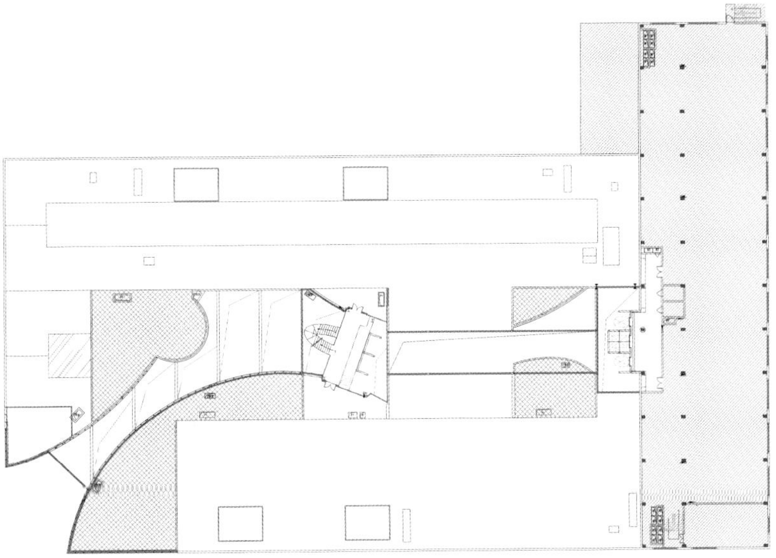

Fourth-floor plan

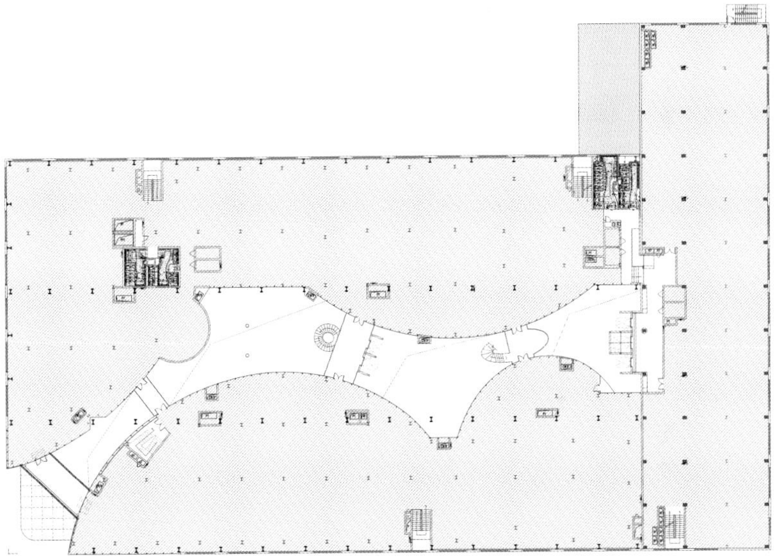

Third-floor plan

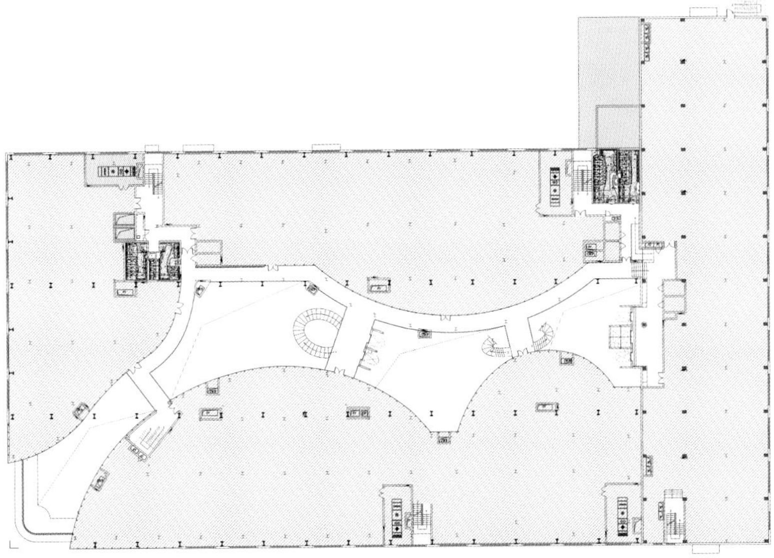

Second-floor plan

The back view of the elevator column

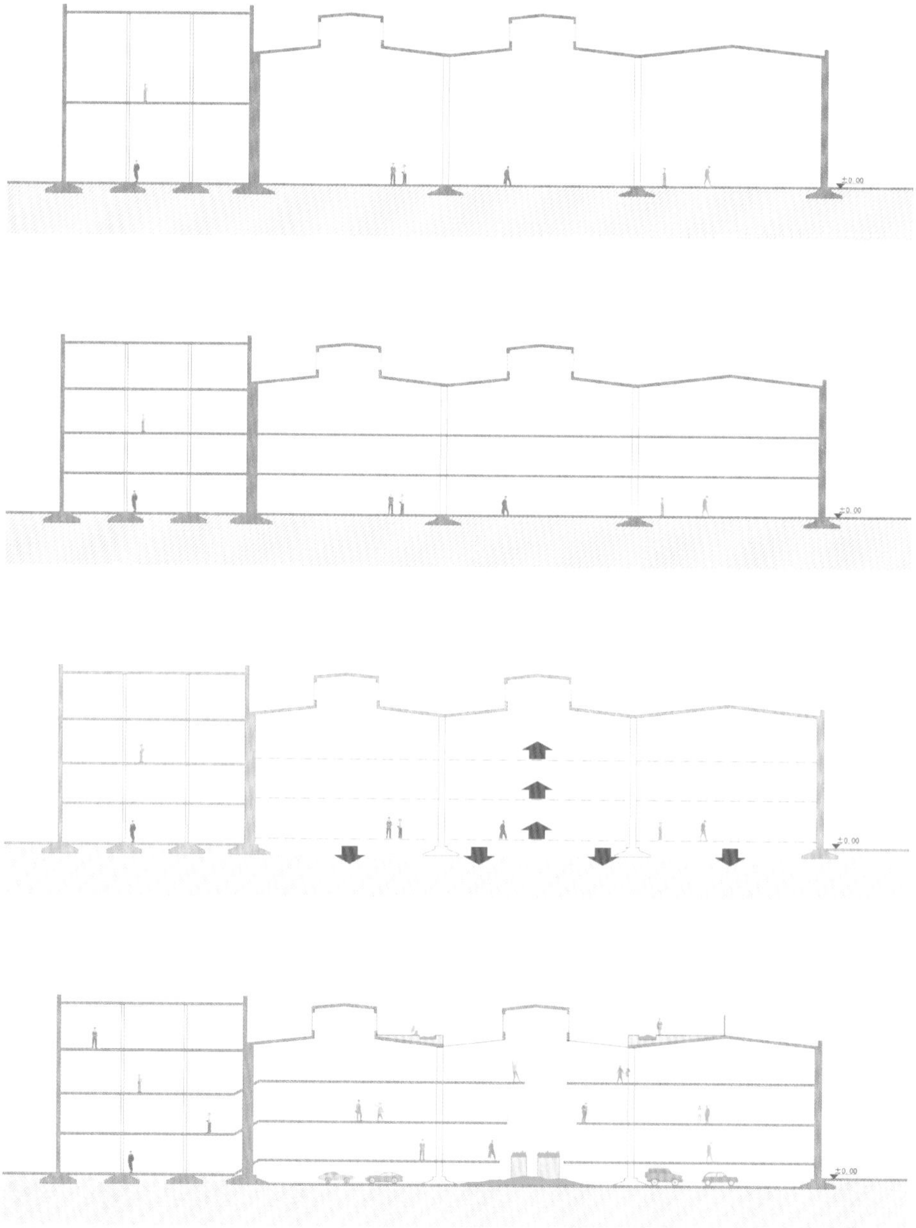

Elevation analysis diagram

TONGJI ARCHITECTURAL DESIGN (GROUP) CO., LTD.

Exterior of the TJAD office building

ABOUT TJAD

Tongji Architectural Design (Group) Co., Ltd. (TJAD), formerly known as the Architectural Design and Research Institute of Tongji University, was founded in 1958 and has now developed into a well-known large-scale design and consulting group.

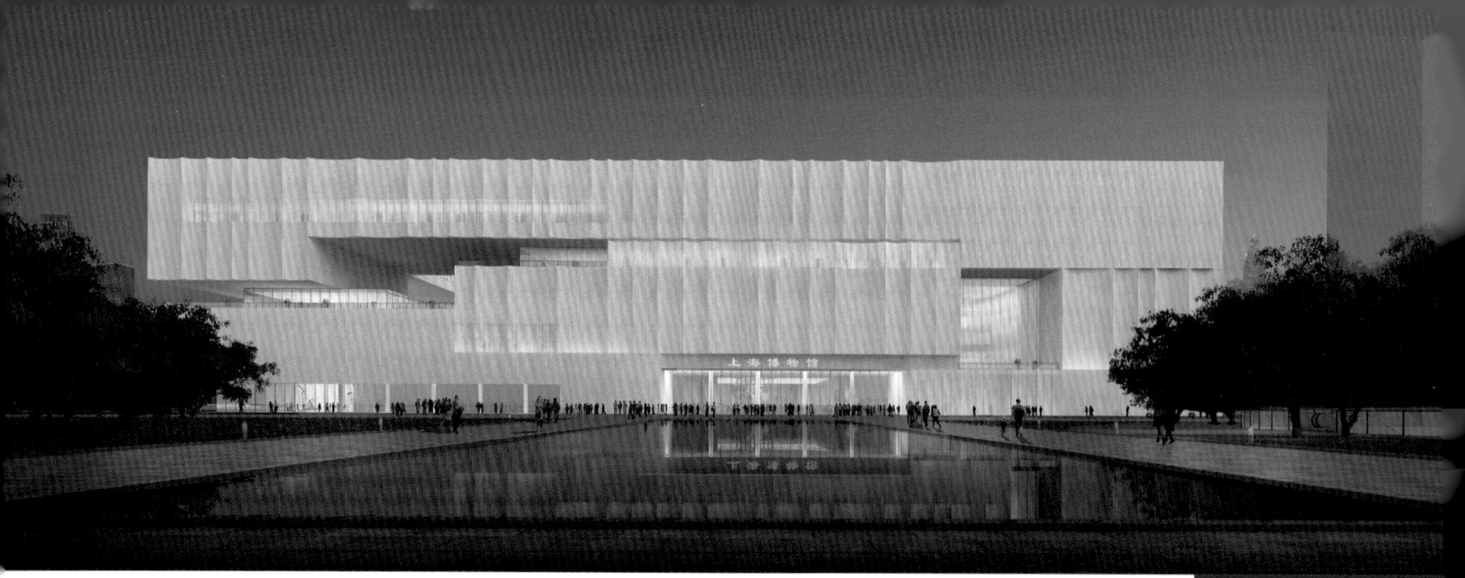

Shanghai Museum East Hall

With almost seventy years of history behind them, and with the profound cultural foundation of Tongji University, TJAD has accumulated a rich experience in both engineering design and technical consultancy, progressing notably over the last sixty-four years. TJAD is a design institution with one of the most extensive design qualifications in China, with a business scope that includes consulting, engineering design, project management, geotechnical engineering, and geological exploration in the fields of building engineering, road engineering, municipal engineering, landscape engineering, environmental pollution prevention, and conservation of historical and cultural relics, among others. The organization has embarked on thousands of projects in China, Africa, and South America that include, among many, Shanghai Tower, Fangfei Garden of the Diaoyutai State Guest House, Table Tennis Gymnasium of the 2008 Olympic Games, African Union Conference Center, New Jinggangshan Revolution Museum, Shanghai Xintiandi, Theme Pavilion of the 2010 Shanghai Expo, Shanghai International Tourist Resort, Shanghai Natural History Museum, Shanghai Symphony Orchestra Concert Hall, China Corporate United Pavilion of Expo 2015 Milan, Havana Hotel of Cuba, Saikang Di Stadium of the Republic of Ghana, the National Arts Center of Republic of Trinidad and Tobago, Sutong Yangtze River Highway Bridge, and Shanghai A5 (Jiading-Jinshan) Expressway Project.

Shanghai Tower
(Cooperative Design,
in partnership with
Gensler, Cosentini, and
Thornton Tomasetti)

Museum of Art Pudong
(Cooperative Design,
in partnership with
Ateliers Jean Nouvel)

Xi'an International Convention and Exhibition Center (Cooperative Design, in partnership with gmp and WES)

TJAD employs more than five thousand outstanding architectural design and engineering personnel to provide top engineering consulting services for our clients, and we have been working hard to promote urban development, so that we may build a better life for citizens through our many professional practices.

We firmly believe that it is the trust that our clients have in us that gives TJAD opportunities to grow. As part of the society and industry, we strive to continue to channel unremitting efforts toward industry development and social progress, just like we have been doing the past sixty-four years.

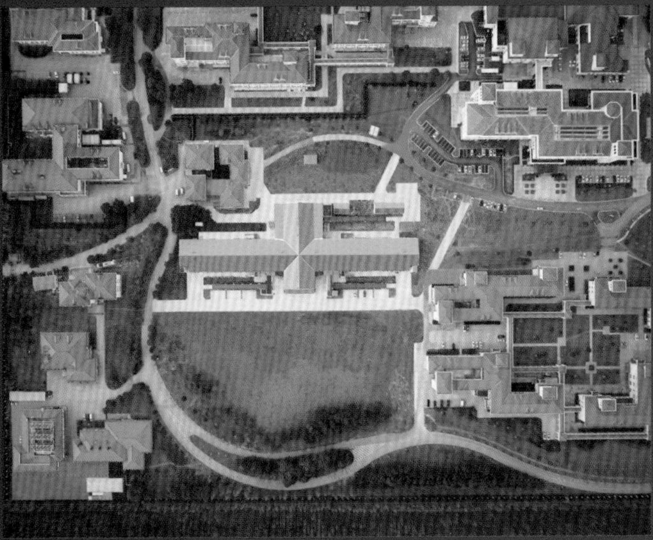

Contingency and Temporary Medical Building of Shanghai Public Health Clinical Center

Shangyin Opera House (Cooperative Design, in partnership with Christian de Portzamparc, Xu-Acoustique, and Theater Projects Consultants)

Green Hill, Shanghai

TONGJI ARCHITECTURAL DESIGN (GROUP) CO., LTD., (TJAD)

同济设计TJAD

VISION

Become a respected design and engineering consultancy with global influence

MISSION

Enable people to live and work in a better place with our creative labor

CORE VALUES

Focus on customers and grow together with employees

SPIRIT

Work together and pursue excellence

Address: No.1230 Siping Road, Shanghai, China, 200092
Telephone: 0086-21-65987788
Email: 5wjia@tjad.cn
Web: www.tjad.cn